IT'S UP TO YOU!

# IT'S
# UP
# TO
# YOU!

## ERNEST HOLMES

### Enlarged and Revised Edition

*Revision by*
## WILLIS KINNEAR

SCIENCE OF MIND PUBLICATIONS
Los Angeles, California

Seventh Printing - November 1983

*Published by* SCIENCE OF MIND PUBLICATIONS
3251 West Sixth Street, Los Angeles, California 90020

# CONTENTS

# FOREWORD

What you experience in your everyday life is largely a matter of your own choice, whether or not you realize it. Sometimes that choice is specifically and consciously made; other times the choice is automatic, being a culmination of habitual patterns of thought and emotion.

However, whatever your lot may be there is always the potential for a greater experience of all those things that make living more worthwhile. The process of achieving an ever greater abundance of the good things of life lies not so much in outward efforts as in an inner process of thought.

It is in your own mind that you create and establish the causes, the patterns, of your daily experience. You may not fully agree with this, but it is nonetheless true. And you will prove it to be so as you come to learn to redirect your thoughts so that they are more affirmative than negative. As you do this every aspect of your experience will change for the better.

In the pages of this book you will find many ideas which will enable you to upgrade your thinking, permit you to discover the pathway to more abundant living, and discover a new joy and vitality in just being alive.

The ideas, the ways and means, are presented to you. What you do with them, how you use them, and what they will mean to you is a very personal matter. If you honestly and sincerely desire to make your life better, the way is open to you.

What you do about it is up to you!

WILLIS KINNEAR

# 1

# ESCAPE TO LIFE

It appears that every individual is afraid of something. Maybe it is only a fear of having people believe we have a fear. Maybe it is only a subjective holdover tendency from our religious forebears who devoutly believed that God must be feared. Maybe it is only the fear of what people will think about us: what we have, what we do, or how we look.

There are various sources from which people derive fear, and there are certain fundamental fears which practically all people have. Let us consider these fears, try to analyze them and see what is behind them, where they come from, and whether or not we shall be able to do anything about getting rid of them.

The fear of death is the Goliath which slays the multitudes. The reason this is such a great fear is not only because we cannot bear the thought of leaving behind the people we love, but because it involves an uncertainty of the future. And this fear of death involves all uncertainty and fear of lack—lack of time, lack of friends, lack of health, and lack of economic security that is one of the greatest fears in the world today.

Where shall we go when we die? This is certainly one of the big questions in our mind. If today is the logical continuance of yesterday, then all the tomorrows that stretch down the vistas of eternity will be a continuity of experience and remembrance. We shall keep on keeping on. We shall continue in our own individual stream of consciousness, but forever and ever expanding. Not less but ever more; more, and still more.

Regardless of all we believe can be accomplished by man because of his oneness with God, I do not believe that any man can be happy unless he believes in the continuity of his own existence. I have come to believe that it is impossible for a man to be contented in this life unless he feels sure of the next one. I believe that the greatest single curative power known to the mind of man is a spiritual thought in the subjective mind. By spiritual thought I mean, here, an absolute inner conviction that one may trust in the integrity of the Universe and that sooner or later all things will be made right. Without that we have materialism, and a philosophy of materialism never yet created a great art, a great religion, a great philosopher, or a great anything.

Man spends the first third of his life in preparing himself for life—physically, mentally, and financially. He is always expecting, hoping, progressing, expanding—something big, something satisfying is going to happen. Consequently, his mind is open. He is happy. He is expressing. During the next third of his life, speaking of the average man, he marries, he has a family. His whole thought and emotion is spent here. But quite frequently, in the last third of his life he begins to meet with frustrations. When the time was that everyone believed in some kind of religion, he trusted to some kind of a future. Now this is more likely than not to be shaken. Dr. Jung, one of the world's greatest psychologists, said: "As a physician I am convinced that it is hygienic—if I may use the word—to discover in death a goal towards which one can strive; and that shrinking away from it is something unhealthy and abnormal which robs the second half of life of its purpose. I therefore consider the religious teaching of a life hereafter consonant with the standpoint of psychic hygiene." And people who do not have it will miss something, because during that last third of life there will be little to which they can look forward. That is why we often see the last third of a man's life appear to decline when it should be another great experience and a subjective preparation for something even more sublime.

The soul longs, with its deepest intensity, for self-preservation. It is the spiritual conviction in that deep cryptic being of ours that we are born of eternal day and made in the image of God to traverse a heavenly way. It is the strongest emotion we have. Why is this true unless way back there, in the beginnings of creation, there was incarnated in us that deathless Principle of Life which of Itself knows no defeat? We may analyze ourselves all we want to, and get a certain satisfaction out of so doing, but there can never còme lasting peace and happiness without spiritual conviction, the reason being that Spirit is Reality.

If a man knows that Life never began and will never end, he will be immediately fortified and inspired to begin the work of bringing out perfection in his daily life. When a man understands that God is incarnated in him; that he is a new creation —an individual impartation of that which is Divine—he feels a new birth. When he grasps the fact that the Divine thing in him which longs to be, will always be, then will his intellect see it and his emotion respond to it and life can no longer frighten him.

There is another fear which is as great as the fear of death, and that is the fear of life—the fear of people, the fear which comes from sensitiveness. In some respects this is the worst

11

fear that can take hold of one. There is probably no way of weighing and measuring it as against other fears, but there is none greater than the fear of life.

Generally speaking, the man who is misunderstood, who is frequently criticized, is likely to be doing something worthwhile. It is the person with whom everyone agrees that is lost in the mass of mediocrity. The head that lifts itself above the others has the rock thrown at it, so we need not be concerned when people criticize us. Of course it is normal to want people to like us, and a good thing to say to ourselves when people criticize us is: "If people knew me better they would like me." This is literally true, for if we could know every man in the right way we would certainly find something in him to admire.

Often the reason we are disturbed when people say unkind things is because we have a sense of our own inadequacy. This can be cured. A bit of conceit would cure it, but that is using one ill to erase another—a counter irritation, like applying a mustard plaster on your neck which burns so that you forget your first pain. Truly speaking, the man with a sense of inferiority and the man who is conceited are alike just mentally sick people. No one is great and no one is small. This is obviously true for every human being has immediate access to Good, by his own acceptance, and every man can have all of It that he can embody.

However, there is nothing objective one can do when suffering from a hurt without becoming arrogant, which the whole world now recognizes as a defense mechanism. Besides, it does no good for in the silence of his own soul the person is still suffering, no matter how arrogant he may appear. That is why we can feel nothing but pity for the sarcastic man. We know that we are looking at a man who is attempting to hide his own hurt.

Naturally we want to get over this feeling hurt, this fear of what other people think about us. How comforting it is to know that we do not have to heal ourselves of what the other man thinks about us or about anyone. We need only to heal ourselves of what *we* think. It can be done. As we come to understand that a man's shortcomings are merely his diseases, like the measles and mumps, just some place that his thinking became warped, we can no more censure him than we would condemn ourselves for holding a distorted viewpoint. And if ever we become so perfect that we do not have any diseases, then we shall never see them in anyone else, and in this conscious unity with our good people will be healed by the very atmosphere of our presence.

As individuals, working out our freedom, we want to get away from argument, from hurts, from trying to force our opinions on others, from pretending, and from the feeling that we have to suffer other people's criticism. This can be done in one, and only one, way: by seeing right through all this camouflage to the eternal Spirit back of each one of us, the One Mind in which we all "live and move and have our being." All are made out of the same Stuff. When we unify, in love, with Life we talk in a universal language with which we can speak to prince or pauper.

Of course we can understand the fear of physical suffering, not only because of the discomfort and pain, but because it disturbs all the normal relationships of life. We shall be able to overcome it when we are positive in our own minds that it is neither intended, Divinely ordained, nor endowed with permanence. Then, and not until then, will we believe we can escape from the bondage of suffering.

I do not know any man who has entirely overcome all the ills of the flesh, but I do know the greatest aid that can come to him is to rid his mind of all fear. Once fear is aroused it dominates the conscious operations of mind and body. We have no fight with doctors, medicine, surgery, or hospitals. We believe in everything that makes for the well-being of man, mentally and physically. Many of the greatest doctors in the world agree with us today that there is not a sick person on earth who would not be far better off if he consciously co-operated with spiritual healing, recognizing the fact that all things are Divine; that each thing in its place is best; and that God uses every avenue for expression.

A hundred years ago it was considered quite the thing for a woman to be "delicate." The greater her opportunities for leisure, the more one heard of her ailments. But the world is changing. Many people now are ashamed to let anyone know when they are ill. They have at least sensed the fact that it is not natural to be sick. And thousands are recognizing, in varying degrees, the necessity of making their minds impregnable to the fear of disease. To many is coming the knowledge and faith that there is a great Power everywhere which works toward good rather than bad. And this is our release: seeing that there is no power in the Universe against us. As God cannot behold evil, it follows He does not know disease. Therefore disease is not a Divine Reality, never was, and never can be. We must conclude, then, that the Great Physician within us that already has created us in His own image and likeness senses us as perfect. And when our sense of that perfection shall be complete, then perfection will be manifest in and through us. This consciousness of the ever-present availability of Good will go a long way toward eradicating the fear of disease.

Another great fear is the fear of want, in all of its ramifications. It is one of the most amazing sights that civilization has ever witnessed that in a land of plenty, filled with abundance, thousands are unable to sleep because of their fear of not having enough to eat, enough to wear, enough with which to pay their rent, and so on. We are neither blaming the rich man because he has more than we, nor are we blaming ourselves that we have less, but we know that when we shall have learned how to live, such a state will not exist again.

Society, thus far, has been subject to want, according to economic cycles, and we may never discover in this life how to live correctly. But when the collective intelligence of the race shall arrive at a concept of freedom, the human race will be free, and not subject to the fear of limitation.

But is there any way that we, as individuals, may learn how to do away with want? I think so. We cannot wait for the world to become happy. Jesus made it plain that the place to begin is in individual consciousness: " . . . cast out first the beam out of thine own eye . . . ." If we do this we do not need to worry about whether or not the world is progressing. All the great stirrings in the world today are the result of a change of thought in one individual first, then his community, then his state, and so on.

If we are thinking clearly we shall know that it is not going to rob anyone else if we have enough. Jesus said that he came that we might "have life . . . more abundantly," and since nature has already provided enough, it must be that when we know how to take it we shall have it. By merging mentally and spiritually into the consciousness that there is enough to go around, we shall overcome the fear of want, and we shall overcome want at the same time because they are one and the same thing—the thought and the image.

We are subject to and the servant of anything that we obey emotionally, and unfortunately our possessions often possess us. If we could only come to know that there is such a thing as spiritual Substance, and that that Substance is limitless and omnipresent and that It takes form in our experience according to the mold we give It, then we would only need to open our consciousness to It and we should be able to demonstrate what we needed. It would be folly to think of saving it, for the supply is ever available. We would then be no more apt to hoard wealth than we are to save the water we failed to drink from a particular glass. We always know we can get more.

The law of nature is use or lose. The people who are truly prosperous are generous souls. Even our intellects become sluggish if unused. Our muscles become flabby from a lack of use. Talents unused seem to disappear. We must bear in mind that there is an inflow and only by permitting an outflow, to pass the blessings on, do we widen the channel for the inflow. This thought alone should cure us of any thought of hoarding.

Jesus lived and taught but his having lived will be no salvation for us unless we go and do likewise. It is only our conscious unity with Good that saves. Abundance will come to every individual when he is wed to it and is conscious of that union. We shall all get over our fear of want when we come to such a consciousness of spiritual Substance that we can know that everything we do brings to us that which we need.

Many people harbor a fear of punishment. Shall we be rewarded for our virtues and punished for our mistakes? I believe that we shall be. But by reward and punishment I do not mean anything other than that sin is a mistake and punishment a consequence. There could not be a God who either rewards or punishes. To believe so would be a concept of dualism, a house divided against itself, a king angry one day and loving the next. Unthinkable! I believe in Law, a Law that governs all things and all people. If we make mistakes, we suffer. We do this right here, now, and shall no doubt do so hereafter. Reward and punishment are the logical outcomes of the uses we make of life. But this problem never enters the mind of one who is at peace with himself and with life.

The first step in overcoming any fear is to concede that God is for us. This done, we have at once overcome the fear by seeing that there is nothing to be afraid of. The world is all right and we can meet it on its own terms, but let us meet it constructively, as a gloriously becoming thing, knowing that the kingdom of God inhabits every soul. No one has ever tried and failed in a conscious cooperation with the Universe Itself.

You are king in the domain of your mind, and the genius of God is under the command of your choice. If you harbor fears, you do it with your eyes open. It's up to you!

# 2

# SUCCESSFUL LIVING

One of the oddest quirks that we discover in human nature is to find someone desiring to be radiantly well, gloriously happy, abundantly supplied, well loved and fully expressed, and yet avoiding any use of the word "spiritual" and shunning any possible thought that he may desire to be known as spiritual. The fact that he is anxious to secure a material fortune but cannot bring himself to connect it with anything spiritual may be a holdover from the old belief that to desire the good things of life, while not exactly sinful, was yet an unworthy ideal. Many wince at the mention of God in connection with supply, as if such a thought were blasphemous.

By spirituality we mean a constructive atmosphere of goodness, truth, beauty, harmony, and reality. Such an atmosphere comes in such degree as one comes to believe, to understand, and to make use of the invisible Presence, the invisible Intelligence, which is what we mean when we speak of the Spirit or God. To be spiritually minded is to be whole-minded. To be whole-minded is to be holy. It means that we realize the complete unity of God and His creation. If we, therefore, demand from ourselves, freely, openly, and emphatically, a spiritual reaction to success, it means that we understand the complete unity and close relationship of all life and can the more fully express prosperity and success.

What do we mean by "success"? A life that is complete. This does not necessarily mean the acquisition of a million dollars. A man might be a millionaire and at the same time a dismal failure. Equally, a man might have a very few dollars and be a rich man because he would be satisfied, happy, complete. Success means that which is necessary to maintain a balance, an equilibrium. Subjectively, it means a state of well-being, a sense of happiness; objectively, an environment that reflects this inner state of consciousness.

A successful man will be at peace, and because he is at peace he will be happy; and because he is happy he will be surrounded by happy circumstances. He will have a sufficient consciousness of substance that his environment will reflect a degree of supply sufficient to enable him to have those things which make for a fuller life, whether we call it much or little. A successful man will have such a consciousness of the unity of good that this consciousness will find its objective correspondent in friendship, in love, in human interest.

The word "poverty" usually conveys to our minds the idea of a money shortage, but actually the word means the lack of any good thing. Poverty is the very antithesis of abundance, and abundance of good is necessary to human happiness. It is only as we experience good that God is expressed through us. The more completely we realize good—in all of its manifold expressions of health, wealth, and happiness—the more completely do we express God; that is, the more does God become personified through us.

If God could know anything of lack or limitation of any kind—lack of money, lack of health, lack of intelligence, lack of friends—then *lack* would be an eternal verity, for God is changeless. What He knows today He has always known, and will know throughout eternity. But God is always One, not a house divided against itself, and He can never know anything unlike Himself, so we need not be concerned about lack ever becoming a Reality.

There is nothing in the Universe that limits us, or that would or could desire to limit us. The idea that God is trying our souls to see whether or not we can take it, so to speak, is nonsense; it is born in ignorance, in superstition, in the nighttime of the soul, and has nothing to do with spiritual realization. There is no power in the Universe that tries or tempts us but our own ignorance. The Universe withholds nothing from us because in withholding It would withhold from Itself, and we are some part of Its purpose. Therefore, not only is there nothing in the Universe that limits or restrains us, but the Spirit even seeks, urges, pushes against us to fulfill Itself. We should get a clear understanding of this, for a man is already defeated if he approaches life with the morbid idea that there is some power ready to deny him or to inflict punishment upon him.

Every normal individual feels that there is Something in the Universe which, if he could get hold of It, would straighten him out. This insistent and universal desire for self-expression which every man feels is proof that there is Something that wants us to be successful. Furthermore, we could not experience such an urge if its fulfillment did not already exist for us in Divine Mind.

It is apparent that man has had the accumulative instinct from the beginning of his history, and Jesus did not denounce this acquisitive faculty, if we use it in connection with the universal Law: " . . . seek ye first the kingdom of God . . . and all these things shall be added unto you." Within this universal Law is included the law of increase, the law of giving and receiving. There is in man an inherent faculty which lays hold of what is its own, and every needed thing will be "added" if we follow the law of righteous accumulation. We should banish forever the idea that man must be poor to be righteous.

If we believe that God cannot know poverty or any kind of lack; that opulence itself should be manifesting freely in our lives, what steps shall we take to bring abundance into the lives of those who are now experiencing poverty? How shall we make two trees grow where one grew before?

To begin with, we are never seeing poverty but the representation of an idea of lack, a symbol of lack which has taken hold of our consciousness. Poverty itself is not a Divine Reality since God cannot know it, and, therefore, it can be changed. Both prosperity and poverty are states of mind. If we desire to erase the thought of poverty we must go back to the thought of prosperity, an affirmation of the allness of Good, the source of which is God. We are confronted with the revealing truth that poverty is lack of knowledge of God. If we had a complete realization of the allness of Good and our oneness with God, we would automatically express abundance.

All truth resolves itself into this self-evident fact, that the Universe must be a self-sustaining and self-perpetuating spiritual order, amply able to provide for Its own needs and to adequately express Its own inherent desires. Man is some part of this Universe. Why then is he limited unless it be that he has contradicted the fundamental Principle of self-existence, and, in ignorance of his true nature, repudiated the greater claim which he might have made upon the Universe?

Prosperity is a state of mind; activity is also a state of mind; and the law of compensation is an invisible but infallible government of Divine order. It is done unto us as we believe, but the belief is largely subjective and we are all more or less marked by the grooves of experience, a large part of them being adverse. Those who wish to experience the supremacy of spiritual thought over apparent material resistance must claim and know, in their own thought, that there is a Divine Intelligence directing them.

We are not struggling toward wealth, then, as such. It would not make us happy. Happiness is an interior quality, a state of being, the result of knowing that in the long run the Divine will win; the knowledge that we can trust the integrity of the Universe. Our good will come to us in such measure as we ourselves measure it out in our own experience.

All that is in the Universe is with us, nothing is against us. Each one of us has access immediately, in our own consciousness, to that absolute, unconditioned Presence which molds and makes things out of Itself by Itself directly becoming the thing It makes. The good which we desire passes out of It, as though it came from the very hand of God, which it does.

But even God cannot give us anything unless we are in a mental condition to receive the gift. The Law cannot do anything for us unless It can do it through us. We live in the midst of eternal good, but it can only be to us what we believe it to be. We stand at the mouth of the river, but we must let down our own bucket if we wish it filled with the pure waters of Reality. It is not enough that this spiritual Substance is everywhere around us and in us. There were thousands in the crowd through which Jesus passed, yet only one woman—she who touched the hem of his garment—received healing. The woman was eager for the blessing and believed she would receive it. Unless we consciously open our minds and recognize our oneness with omnipresent Substance, we shall appropriate none of It. The knowledge that God wants us to live fully; the certainty that there is no force to keep our good from us; the assurance that abundance is ours for the asking, will avail us nothing unless we use that knowledge.

Those who deny the possibility of Divine guidance have not thought the matter through to its final conclusion. The Universe would be incomplete if man were not expressed. That Principle which so lavishly distributes the heavenly bodies, peopling the infinite reaches of space with personifications of Itself, must have both the intelligence and the ability to provide for man's needs. How can we deny ourselves the privilege of Its personal attention? Some will say that such an infinite Presence cannot be personal. Here again this attitude of mind has not contemplated the full measure of Reality. The Spirit personifies in and through everything—the rose, the blade of grass, the mineral, animal, and human kingdoms. Each and all are specific demonstrations of the ability and desire of universal Mind to find concrete expression.

It is a mistake to suppose that some things are spiritual while others are material, and that a sharp line can be drawn between Spirit and matter. There is no variation in the spiritual Principle which underlies and governs all expression. Matter is Spirit in form; conditions, Spirit in many forms. The best business methods evolved for the handling of affairs are the ones nearest Truth. All legitimate business, constructively handled, is in accord with Truth. The Spirit expresses Itself in everything, since God is All-in-All, and there is no dividing line between form and substance.

While we know that our business is an activity of the Spirit working through us, we shall be viewing our business in the right light. When we are certain that the things in which we are interested are constructive, we should go ahead with complete assurance of success. The only Power there is is with us, for there is no power opposed to the Truth.

23

In our spiritual mind treatments for prosperity we resolve things into ideas, conditions into states of thought, and act upon the premise that the thought is the father of the thing. This method is both direct and effective, and when rightly used becomes a law unto the thing thought of.

But in doing this we often contact obstacles in our thought which rob us of our good. For instance, we sometimes come up against the thought of competition, the belief that there are too many people engaged in the business in which we are interested. Competition is a belief that there is not enough good to go around, and while believed in this thought manifests itself in limitation. In other words, if we feel that our line of business is crowded, and we must therefore be on tiptoe to keep ahead of the other fellow, the probabilities are that we will find ourselves crowded out. We must resolve this thought into its native nothingness. Truth does not compete with anyone. Therefore, we should not allow the thought to enter our minds that we are competing with anyone. We should never watch to see what another is doing or how he is doing it, for when we do this we are limiting our own possibilities to the range of another's vision. Principle is not bound by precedent, and our good is not limited or conditioned by any good that has ever been manifest. We should confidently expect a greater good than we have ever experienced, or than we have ever known of anyone experiencing.

In everyone there is a unique possibility, ready to take the stamp of his individuality, and anyone who has not yet discovered his particular niche in the scheme of things should work more for direction and guidance than for the demonstration of prosperity. He robs no man who takes his place in the rightful scheme of creation, and, fulfilling his own destiny, becomes a beacon light that others, seeing his light, may find the way again. To believe in competition is altogether false and untrue. There is plenty to go around, with an abundance left over. As Emerson said: "Men suffer all their life long, under the foolish superstition that they can be cheated. But it is as impossible for a man to be cheated by any one but himself, as for a thing to be and not to be at the same time." When the mental gate which is now obstructing the flow of Spirit through the uniqueness of our individuality is lifted, there will be an outpush which nothing can resist. Every man should be willing and happy to be himself, remembering that "imitation is suicide."

Will power has nothing whatever to do with success or prosperity. The abundant life is the result of the operation of Law. We cannot conceive of any amount of will power having anything to do with two and two making four. All the will we need is the knowledge that they do make four. So we must come into the knowledge that we are surrounded by a spiritual Law which receives the impress of our thought and acts upon it creatively and intelligently. If we act in accordance with Law, there is nothing that can withhold our good from us. If we fail—well, that is our affair. The Universe knows nothing about negation and God does not know about our failure. The secret of getting what we want lies in using the Law governing what we want.

Ideas come from infinite Mind through what we call the human mind. But ideas can only come to the mind that expects them and opens its doors of thought so they can enter and pass through into expression. A man, before he can be truly successful, must be spiritual-minded, without longing to die and go to heaven. In other words, he must begin to consciously experience spirituality while in the flesh. It is asking a lot of ourselves, but not one-half of what the Universe intends for us. Nothing will be lacking in our world when we recognize our spiritual inheritance. "He that hath a bountiful eye, shall be blessed . . . ." We fulfill the law of increase by seeing with the bountiful eye.

3

# YOU CREATE YOUR DESTINY

One of the greatest stumbling blocks in any man's spiritual advancement is dishonesty: the refusal to honestly face an idea if that idea happens not to please him. This comes in part from the human tendency to take the line of least resistance, whether it be in our physical endeavors or in the operation of our mind. Confronted with an idea that repudiates one we have held for years, we go far out of our way, entirely around the idea, to keep from being compelled to analyze and possibly to absorb it. Our cry is: "I do not like to believe that!"

Back of this is the fear that an idea may be forced into our consciousness which will uncover to us our own responsibility. If we are falling behind in the race of life we do not like to think it is our fault. If we are experiencing physical discomfort we attribute it to the weather, to long hours of work, to inherited tendencies toward certain diseases, to the food we eat —to anything rather than to the ideas we have entertained. If we seem less successful than our neighbor (and it seems difficult for us not to compare ourselves with some neighbor, absurd as it is) we say to ourselves, "It is because I did not have as good a start in life"; "It is because he has a pull that I do not have," or some other excuse equally as ridiculous, rather

27

than face the fact that we are the actual creators of our own destiny. We do not like to believe that.

Every normal-minded person believes in something greater than himself. Every scientific person is compelled to admit that there is an Intelligence in the Universe, whether or not he ascribes the elements of personality to It. It is not a mark of intelligence to deny a supreme Something. There is an absolute and positive Presence to which we may consciously come and which will consciously respond to us. This universal Presence does not bless some and damn others, but responds to everyone who approaches It.

We have a right to believe this for the simple reason that we can talk to one another and be understood by one another. So far as we understand the law of intelligence we may set it down as axiomatic that intelligence responds to intelligence, intelligently. If this is true of man, the part, why is it not true of the Whole? Universal Intelligence, if It exists, must respond to us. God is more than an infinite It, more than a cold Principle without any motivation of feeling and emotion.

When we are told there is no such thing as an individual good; that as we claim great ability, great opportunities, great happiness, we are recognizing these things for every man whose consciousness is open to receive them, perhaps we say, "I do not like to believe that." Maybe we think the other man can attend to his own business; he can make his own affirmations of good. He can. But all blessings that we claim as belonging to us, as perfect man, are also the qualities of real man everywhere. All blessings from God are as impersonal as the sun and rain. The soil will produce just as beautiful strawberries for the man in the next town as it will for you and me, if that man uses correctly the law governing the planting of strawberries.

If you tell me about the beauties of some mountain scene I have never experienced, I get from you a word picture but I do not have the thing in the same way that you have it. It is now yours, and when I experience it, it is mine. Why, then, may we not feel justified in believing that the universal Mind is at this moment all around us and within us, and as we wake up to a perception of Its presence It wakes up to us, so to speak, and flows in us and through us. In such degree as we embody It, It embodies us.

We all look about us and discover we have a certain physical environment. We may like it or we may not like it. We may think it is beautiful or we may think it is ugly. We may say it is friendly or we may say it is not friendly. But regardless of this, each one's environment is going to be to him what he is to it. Obviously, God could not create man with the gift of free choice without making him able to think, and he cannot think without bringing upon himself the results of his thinking. Universal Mind has no choice but to create through Law the thought that is given to It. If It could contradict that thought It would be recognizing something outside of Itself and would not be a unity. There is nothing which we see in the entire universe, whether it be a tree, a stove, a man, or a bird, other than a thought objectified. It could not be there if it were not made out of Mind, for that is all there is to make anything out of.

That our thought is creative should be the most comforting idea ever entertained by us because with it comes the realization that it is creative only because we are using the Mind of God. What greater concept can ever come to us than the realization that God is with us? " . . . If God be for us, who can be against us?" To the man who will take the position that he wishes to work in union with the Power of Good, will come all the power that he can conceive of, and accept. Such a man will then know that he cannot fail in what he really wants to do.

It is not a matter of whether we call God the Spirit or Mind or the creative Principle or the universal Mind or the heavenly Father or something else. One thing we must learn is that it does not matter what we call anything; the only thing that matters is that we have the right idea about the things to which we give a name. The Divine Reality responds alike to the symbol of the cross or the crescent. We should think of our spirit as being part of the universal Spirit, and of our mind as open to the Divine influx. As any specific knowledge must come from the center of all knowledge, it follows that whenever and wherever the mind of man is open to the Divine influx, it will receive instructions directly from the Source of all. Science, invention, art, literature, philosophy, and religion have one common center from which is drawn all knowledge.

But we must not overlook what we term negative thoughts: thoughts of hate, of lack, of jealousy, of greed. Creative Law takes these and gives them back to us, multiplied. Undoubtedly we do not like this. We are perfectly willing to concede that we help ourselves somewhat by uplifting thoughts. Maybe we go so far as to admit that spiritual thought is creative. But negative thoughts—surely they have no power to do anything? Just the power that we give them. The creative Law cannot refuse to fill the form that our thoughts give It. It does not know "good" or "bad" thoughts; It knows only to multiply and return to us that which we create in our thought. We cannot hinder the Law. We cannot express freedom when we are in bondage to negative beliefs. We had better respect the action of the Law if we expect perfect results. When confronted with undesirable conditions—inharmony and lack—we know they are the result of improper use of the Law. We know we have been betrayed by an erroneous thought, and we will not allow any self-righteousness to dull our ability to separate the real from the false. We will declare our unity with Good and know that the Law of our being is a law of annihilation to anything unlike Itself.

We must remember that we are not dealing with a field about which we can say I do, or do not, like to believe thus and so. It is not a question of likes and dislikes. It is only a question of what is so and what is not so.

Our body—the objective manifestation of the invisible Principle of Life—is always an effect. It cannot by any possibility be a cause. So, if we would change conditions in the body, our only alternative is to go back to the cause in mind and make the change there.

When we speak of the body of a man's affairs, we refer to the outward condition of his circumstances. His business or his environment, which is always an effect of his inner life, can be changed by changing the thought about the conditions. God does not bestow the gift of abundance upon this or that man. God does not know whether you and I have much or little. The Source of our supply is unlimited and it rests with us how much we will embody.

Every time we say that our environment is against us, we are cursing it and cursing ourselves in our relationship to it. Let us erase any thought of hate—the tare of the wheat, the devil grass of the lawn. Let us pull it up and leave only thoughts of right action. Let us bless our environment, visualize it as ideal in thought and imagination. We should mentally create an environment which is more like that which we feel will make us happy. The existence of life is from within and never from without. The environment should be contemplated as full of joy, love, appreciation, and recognition. People often say, "I do this or I do that and am never paid for it." It is impossible for a man to be compensated for his work if he refuses to be compensated. If we contemplate our environment as not appreciating us, then we shall get back from it in kind —we will not be paid.

We should convince ourselves that it is as important to comply with the Law on the unseen side of life as it is to abide by law in the manifest world. If you were given a recipe for a cake that you had particularly enjoyed and you prepared to bake one just like it, would you, with all the ingredients before you and the recipe in your hand, say, "I am not going to put in any flour. I do not like flour. I do not like to believe that flour should go into this cake"? Your own sanity would prevent that. You would know there were certain standards that you must live up to if you hoped to produce a cake of the kind and quality you had in mind.

If you drive an automobile you would not say, "Today I am going to drive this car without gas. I do not like the smell of gas. I do not like to think this car requires gas in order to run." If you were in your car and attempting to operate it in this manner you would probably be sent to the nearest psychopathic ward. Yet, knowing that Law is God's method of operation, that Law obtains throughout all nature, governing both the seen and the unseen, we insist on doing things in our own way simply because we like it better. Will we like the results better?

Heretofore maybe we have been unconscious creators, so let us not condemn ourselves. When we perfectly understand the Law and work with It we shall be able to bring into our lives the good that we wish. Let us accept this power, with love and gratitude, and start to create a more wonderful destiny for ourselves.

# 4

# WHO ARE YOU?

For almost two thousand years this question has been reverberating through the halls of time: "Whom say ye that I am?" And equally long we have been proving how little we knew about the correct answer. The requests that have been made "in the name of Christ" are so foreign to Jesus' nature that they reveal, with the clearness of a polished mirror, how little we have glimpsed of our real heritage.

In studying the life and teachings of Jesus, the most unique character in history, we discover a few simple ideas underlying his philosophy, the embodiment of which enabled him to become the Christ. Fundamental to his concept of life was his belief in a universal Spirit, which he called God or the heavenly Father. This heavenly Father was an Intelligence to which he consciously talked and from which, undoubtedly, he received a definite reply.

This whole philosophy, spiritually conceived, is based on the assumption that such a Reality exists, that standing within and back of each one of us is God, the eternal Presence as us; that there is nothing between us and It but our belief. Therefore, the thesis is that every man is God, though in the germ; that within the most humble of us stands the personification of the Almighty; and that as much of this as we loose, through right knowing, constitutes spiritual Power. That is what is practiced.

What we are trying to do is so simple that we do not believe that it is true. Jesus said, "Believe!" Believe what? Believe that I am I. Therefore, everyone must turn to himself and believe that he is the direct representation of God on this earth. Man can commune with the Eternal because the other side of man's nature *is* Eternal, and this side, the transitory form in which he molds it, is the use that he is making of the other side. Thus we need to change our mode of thought and try to adjust it to this Divine Ideal which has power, just as the light has power over darkness, because where the light is there is no darkness at all.

John the Baptist, still thundering his message of repentance, could not quite understand this man Jesus who preached the Oneness of God and man. The disciples only vaguely sensed the messages he tried to crowd into the brief time he had with them. But the Gospels, taken in their entirety, give us a clear picture of the Christ—a story of the unfoldment of personality through the experience of one who was aware of his relationship to the universal Spirit.

Jesus thought of the Spirit as being personal to him, as directly responding to and being aware of man's approach to It. No wonder John the Baptist was puzzled! This was certainly not what he had been taught. Most people believed and taught that God was a mandatory power, sitting somewhere in the vastness of space and governing the world with a rod of iron, blessing some and cursing others. Intelligent people of this generation no longer believe that.

Nor did Jesus believe it ages ago. He located God in his own soul. And so complete was this realization that he was unable to find a place where the man Jesus began and God left off, or where the Being of God began and Jesus ceased. This overwhelming conviction of Jesus—the discovery of himself—was the greatest discovery of all time. And in this location of the real Self he unveiled the mystic Christ, heralded throughout the ages as the one anointed of the Most High, the Son of God. This Divine Incarnation is not a historical event; it did not take place two thousand years ago in Judea; it is eternally taking place. That is why Eckhart, the great German Catholic mystic, said that God never had but one Son but the Eternal is forever begetting the Only Begotten. This is just another way of saying: All through the ages God is forever reproducing Himself through humanity, and all humanity is the Sonship. There is but one Son and this is Christ, and as this nature arouses in us, then " . . . the words that I speak unto you, they are spirit, and they are life."

We do not suggest to a person that he is all right when he is not all right. We try to awaken man to an inherent Divinity and Perfection which is in every living soul. Our whole process is an awakening. The spiritual nature never sleeps and something in you and in me senses this "imprisoned splendour" as something that has never been hurt, confused, sick, or poor. Our knowledge of this Divine Reality, according to an immutable Law in the universe, automatically sets the objective man free.

Most of us are running hither and yon searching for Reality outside of ourselves, when all the while the conscious realization of this inner Divinity is the unveiling of the Christ. It is indwelling as well as overdwelling, and the Christ is forever infolded within human personality. The search for Reality must eventually end in the realization that It is within. And he who seeks the Christ outside himself will never find It.

Sooner or later we must come to the conclusion that that which we look for, we look with, and that which we find, we take with us in the search.

Jesus taught, again and again, that whatever is true of man —of the reality of his nature—is the Divine Presence within him. Added to this unique realization, this enlightening concept of Deity, of placing God at the center of his own being, was the realization of an absolute Law obeying his will when his will was in harmony with the Spirit of Truth. Logical and reasonable as this may seem to us now, when Jesus taught this philosophy, this concept of the relationship between God and man, his utterances were novel, to say the least.

We must believe that Jesus was like other men, both humanly and Divinely speaking; so we must conclude that the difference was not in his nature but in the way he used his powers of mind and spirit. But Jesus had an enlightenment which, perhaps, no other man has had before or since his time. He perceived on the one hand a universal Presence, an Intelligence with which he could converse and from which he could draw inspiration and power; and, on the other hand, a Law which he could command and which must obey when his will was in harmony with the Divine Will. Thus Jesus had balanced the meaning of the two pillars which stood in front of the temple of Solomon: the Law and the Word, the relationship between the personal and the impersonal elements of nature. Consequently, there was ever at the door of his thought a Divine inflow of ideas and a dynamic outflow of spiritual Power.

Jesus laid down no hard and fast rules of conduct. His philosophy was one of simplicity: a direct approach to God through our own natures, an abiding faith in Good as the eternal Reality, and an implicit trust in the Law as being absolute. But, at the same time, he made it plain that salvation is not in the wayshower, but in that which is shown; that no man will ever enter the kingdom of heaven by proxy but can enter only by making his unity with Good. While proclaiming this definite relationship between God and man he definitely taught that all men are alike. He said in substance: "If you will listen to what I have been telling you; if you will believe the kingdom of heaven is within you; if you will believe that God is in his kingdom, then will Christ dwell with you." And Jesus *believed* what he taught. That his faith was justified by his works is shown in the results of his life upon the centuries following him.

Always when there dawns upon any individual member of the human race the realization of his own Divinity, the eternality of his own nature, the unity of his own life with the Eternal, and the immediate availability of the Law through the power of his own word—there Christ is born again.

God has not made *some* men Divine, but God has made *all* men Divine, by the very reason of the fact that all men are some incarnation of the Divine Spirit. The same Life runs through all, from the least to the greatest, threading Itself into the patterns of our individualities. Christ, the perfect man, is developed within us through the realization and revelation of the self to the self. God in us is Christ, and Christ in us constitutes our true Sonship to the Parent Mind which is God. So that which Jesus did, we can do. That should not sound sacrilegious except to a person whose mental gates are still closed. When they mistook Jesus for God, he said, in essence: "It is expedient that I go away; you are mistaking a person for a principle, but the Spirit of Truth shall awaken in you the truth which I have been talking about."

Who is there that at times has not felt this inner Presence, this inner sense of a greater Reality which bears witness to Itself through our highest acts and our deepest emotions? In the long run each will fully express his Divinity, for the urge to unfold is constant and unremitting. And the voice of Truth is insistent. Mingled with the voice of humanity is the Word of God, for Truth is a synonym for God. And whoever speaks the Truth speaks the Word of God. Behind all revelation, behind all experience, is a unity; through all is a diversity; and saturating all is a Divinity. The intellect must give its consent and the mind must unify with the Spirit, for the outlet for Truth must be true. And the Christ which Jesus revealed, and is already incarnated in our own natures, seeks to find circumference through our lives.

The more one senses the Universality of things, the more universal the individual mind becomes, the more individual it *can* become, the more one has with which to individualize that Universality. Why? Because the principle of individualism is inherent in the more impersonal presence of that which is universal. That is why Jesus, a man who recognized spiritual Reality, would naturally seek the kingdom of Good first, and then all these things would be added, because the lesser has to be included in the greater. This thought of universal Life being manifest directly through each one of us in a unique way is a very beautiful conception, for if it is true—and there seems no doubt that it is—then there is no one who ever took our place, or ever can, or ever will. There is no one living, no one who ever did live or ever will live, who can do just exactly what we can do in the same way. This knowledge should immediately cure the belief of either an inferiority or a superiority complex.

While every man can say to himself: "There is no living soul that can do what I can do," he should not say it as though he were conceited, for he should at the same time have to remember that every other man can say the same thing to himself. No man can take another's place because the Eternal has put the imprint of individualization of Itself in everyone. Every man is a genius in his own way and need not wonder whether or not his genius will find expression. Emerson said that when we realize our Divine individuality, then the very act creates the outlet for that act. For each one of us could then demonstrate his place in life where he is fulfilled, where he is happy, and as he draws upon the invisible Presence he is drawing upon an infinite Source of inspiration. Jesus understood this perfectly, therefore he put off the old man—the carnal, human, finite conception of limitation—and emerged with the mind of Christ.

Regardless of what opinions we hold, there are only three ways by which knowledge can come to the world. One is science, the result of which is facts. Another is opinion, the result of which is philosophy. The other is illumination, the result of which is religion. From one or all of these three sources all knowledge must come. The great scientists reveal a universal Cause, acting as absolute and immutable Law. The great opinions of philosophy reveal, or should reveal, a reasonable background for self-existent Life. The great religions reveal, or should reveal, a Divinity that shapes our ends. We need all three. Fact will never contradict faith when we place fact and faith in a right relationship to each other. Therefore, the great mystics have never said anything that contradicted the slightest fact. Nor did Jesus deny the experience of people whom he healed. He did not say to them, "Nothing ails you," any more than we would repeat such a nonsensical statement today to people who ask for relief from their suffering.

Jesus recognized that disease was not a necessity and knew

that the sufferer did not have to endure his pain. But Jesus never said "Peace" when there was no peace. While the idea of Christ, implying the concept of Sonship, was more completely manifest in Jesus than in any man who has ever lived, the Christ has come with varying degrees of power to some people in every age, and to every person in some degree.

The recognition of the birth of the Christ consciousness in the individual makes possible a greater experience of the Divine Incarnation. But that birth, as Eckhart said, is forever going on. The expansion is gradual but eternal. What we will be millions of years from now we cannot even guess. We have nothing in our intellect now equivalent to an embodiment of an idea that will even make it significant to us. But this concept of the immediate relationship of the Universal to the individual must always deliver a power to the individual which is commensurate with the concept. The meaning of Christ, then, is the entire creation of God, of which we are a part, a universal demand which the Infinite makes upon Itself that It shall be expressed.

"But whom say ye that I am?"

"Thou art the Christ."

# 5

# THE REAL "YOU"

Someone has said that half a loaf is better than no bread, and ignorant faith is better than no faith. So perhaps we made some progress when our religious convictions were rooted in the Divine even when we were convinced that Divinity was outside of, and vastly removed from, us.

For the first time in the history of human thought we are coming to the place where intelligent people are setting about to rediscover man. People are becoming afraid of what the intellect, uncontrolled by spiritual ideals, may do to the human race. Many modern scientific men are endeavoring, with great earnestness, to find something that gives value to life other than the mere uncovering of mechanical force and energy. Too much knowledge with too little wisdom is dangerous.

If a man is seeking God, and if he happens to have the ability to think straight through, he will arrive at the inevitable conclusion that the discovery of God will have to come through the discovery of himself. This calls for an absolute unity between God and man, not a unity some day to be attained, but one that exists now, that existed before he found it out, and would have existed just the same if he had never made the discovery. Thus we realize that man is immortal now, whether he knows it or not. If this were not true there is nothing he could do to achieve immortality.

As man mentally retraces his steps to the Source of his being—God—there gradually awakens in his consciousness a concept of himself which is transcendent of the objective form. Every individual who lives finds that the great within of himself is immersed in God and *is* God, even though the mental makeup of himself is largely the result of his experience. His physical makeup is merely an image cast as a reflection into the mirror of his experience. Man walks back and forth, enslaved by the shadows of the walls he has cast between himself and Reality. The shackles are phantoms; they are not real and the Truth alone has the power to strike them from him.

It is upon the belief that man is an incarnation of God, and because he is his life is endless, that the whole structure of Christianity is built. And it is upon the same structure that every other great religion the world has ever known has been built. It is upon this inspiration that the greatest poems have been penned. And it is upon this cornerstone that our greatest art has been given to the world.

We have been so afraid of mentioning the word God, so superstitious about everything concerning the Deity, that the thought of ourselves as Divine has been foreign to the general conception. But we have to face facts. We must be honest in our investigation if we are to get anywhere. And if there is anything that we need to know it is this: that the Eternal is incarnated in each one of us; that God Himself goes forth anew into creation through each one of us; and, in such degree as we speak the Truth, the Almighty has spoken. Once we gain this heavenly vision of our Divine Sonship we should claim our Divinity; demonstrate It every day of our life and refuse to make the slightest concession to appearances.

The old idea that the substance out of which our bodies are made is any different from any other substance is an antiquated theory. We now deal with the universe on the basis of an absolute, fundamental, universal unity. The answer of modern science relative to what we have miscalled a "material universe" is that the Universe is One. Science is unifying matter; psychology is tending to unify mind, and we announce that Spirit is One. We think of all mind as One Mind and all spirit as One Spirit.

There is no world external to consciousness, and we shall never know any God greater than the God our inner consciousness proclaims. Look into your own mind and determine whether this is so. This has to be the ultimate criterion because the Universe is to you and to me what we are to It and can never be anything else. Whatever this Life Principle is that animates us, we did not make It. When we speak of God as Causation or Reality, we are not trying to introduce a new fashion. We are referring to a Principle resident within us which we did not put there. No experience we ever had put It there, and certainly all our experiences merely tend to awaken us to the conclusion that It is there and teach us how to use It.

Does God know me? Sooner or later we all ask that question. Either there is no power, no intelligence, nothing in the Universe that knows me or cares what happens to me, or else there is such a Power, omnipresent. It is the all of you, the all of me. But, does It know me? Does It know you? Does It know Itself?

These are deep questions. In the long run each must answer them for himself. I believe that infinite Intelligence does know us, but I do not believe that It knows us apart from Itself. I think we are part of Its Self-knowingness. Therefore I believe that our self-knowingness, what we know about ourselves that is really true, is the present level of our evolution—our present consciousness of God.

In saying this I hasten to explain that I do not think I am God. There is a vast difference between saying I am God and saying God is what I am. Ice is water. All ice is some water, but not all water is ice. So we might say about the life of man: all of the life of man is some of the Life of God; some of the Life of God is all of the life of man, but man is not all of the Life of God.

Certainly we could not pick out any John Jones and say to him, "You are God." But reason does compel us to say to a John Jones, "God is you; there is no you outside of God." If God is a Divine Presence, omnipresent, then it follows that God is present where I am, or there could be no where I am or else the where I appear to be is a hole in the universe. Therefore, if I am, God is that which I am, though of course infinitely more. This is not a question of opinion; it is not so because we think it is so; it is so because it is so. We should not argue as to whether or not we are Divine, but instead gratefully express our Divinity from this moment on, remembering the words of Jesus: "At that day ye shall know that I am in my Father, and ye in me, and I in you."

There is an infinite Intelligence which gives birth to our minds, and if our minds are in league with It, then we arrive at the reason for the power of thought. Does it not follow that the creative power of thought does not repose in the human will, but in the Divine Presence? And should we not have an entirely different conception of spiritual healing if we knew that it had nothing to do with mental suggestion, but with that silent recognition of the Spirit already resident and inherent in the individual for whom we are working? You and

I, by taking thought, do not do anything other than line our-selves up with that which is the Father of thought. But could it be other than that "the highest God and the innermost God is One God"? When we seek to heal spiritually we are seeking to release the spiritual Principle inherent within the individual needing healing.

There is one ultimate Thinker, yet this Thinker thinks through all of us. That is why our thought is creative. That is why we think at all. The universal Mind is incarnated in every-one. Every man has access to It; every man uses It, either in ignorance or in conscious knowledge. In other words, the mind of each one of us is the Mind of God functioning at the level of our perception of life. Consciously using It, we bring into our experience today something we did not appear to have yesterday—a better environment, a happier circumstance, more friendship, more joy. These manifestations are of the nature of Reality.

Is there any danger in teaching a man the truth about him-self? I think not, for when I know that the God in you is the God that is in me—the only reality there is between us—in such degree as I know it I cannot seek to do you ill. It would be unthinkable, because I would know that all I could do would be to hurt myself. The only danger to any man lies in a too rapid intellectual progress without a balance of the spiritual qualities which alone can synthesize. When all the nations of the world shall see God incarnated in each other, then we shall no longer have use for weapons, but it is going to be hard for us to get spiritual realization while we believe that perhaps we are holier than other men.

If we insist on believing that God is somewhere apart from us, or somewhere apart from the person or situation for which we spiritually treat, then how are we going to know whether

God is going to come down and incarnate? But if, on the other hand, we are certain that God is incarnated, it is merely a matter of God in us greeting God in the other person. It is the salutation of the Divine to Itself. That is exactly what self-realization is: the pronouncement of Spirit Itself, the self-announcement of Reality through us.

God in us, as us, is that which we are. The more careful the analysis, the more complete the conclusion has to be that this is so. If this be true, and our mind does partake of that universal Wholeness and is creative, then we are bound by our own liberty, and bondage is an expression of freedom—man's freedom under the infinite Law of all life.

We must not be disturbed by the contradiction of objective experience. We shall have to know that the Truth we announce is superior to the condition which it is to change. We shall have to see that God in us recognizes God in the other person until the God in the other person recognizes God in us. This cannot be done by the human will. It is only when we recognize the pure essence of the spiritual Principle inherent and incarnate in each one of us, that we find that the thought arising from the atmosphere of spiritual realization has no adversary.

Each one of us, in turning to the great inner life, is turning to God. He who penetrates this inner life will find it birthless, deathless, fearless, eternal, happy, perfect, complete. Gradually there dawns in his consciousness a sense that God, or the Infinite, is flowing into everything he is doing.

When is man Divine? The Apostle John answered this question: "Beloved, now are we the sons of God, and it doth not yet appear what we shall be: but we know that, we shall be like him; for we shall see him as he is."

6

# YOUR PERSONALITY

If a person who thought he was unattractive were asked why he felt that way, he might reply that it was because of some physical defect, or because he was too fat or too thin, too tall or too short, or any plausible idea that might suggest itself to him—none of which would be the real reason. And anyone who says he does not care whether or not he is attractive is merely being psychically defiant to fool himself. Every man and woman in the world, given the choice, would be attractive because all the world is seeking happiness. Wealth alone does not bring it; neither fame nor prestige alone will guarantee happiness; no kind of eminence insures it. Only love brings happiness and being attractive is one dependable manner of giving direction, impulse, and momentum to love.

Every person *can* be attractive. Not by the application of external methods, but by thinking on the qualities that make for attraction which will provide a mental equivalent, and attractiveness will then become manifest in his life. Whatever we can make real in thought, provided our thought shall believe it is real, in truth must be real. This is not as easy as it sounds, and yet it is so simple that wise people are confounded by it.

What do we mean by attractive? By this we do not wish to convey the more familiar synonymous terms of ability to allure, to draw, to influence, to entice, but rather the more comprehensive idea of spiritual magnetism—the drawing power of Spirit, which is forever irresistible.

The effort to acquire an attractive personality need not be accompanied by a tumultuous cataclysm. It requires only that we become wisely fastidious in the choice of our mental diet, realizing that we will starve our higher nature by giving living quarters to negative thoughts—such as the belief that we are unattractive—whereas thoughts on the supremacy and allness of Mind will nourish and exalt us. When we understand this thoroughly, we will no more indiscriminately accept the vagrant thoughts that hover about our mental doorway than we would indiscriminately accept any unchoice food that was placed before us.

There are certain points relative to the meaning of the life of the individual which appear so self-evident that it would be impossible intelligently to maintain a denial of them: first, that there is a Creativeness in the Universe which gives rise to the creativeness in the individual, therefore that the Creativeness in the Universe and the creativeness in the individual is the same Creativeness. Second, that there is in the Universe, and in the individual, a personal element which makes possible free will, self-choice, spontaneous action, restricted only to the necessity of such volition forever remaining true to the natural order of things and to the nature of Reality.

When an understanding of these two points has become a part of our conscious belief we will understand how natural it is for an idea held in mind to become manifest in our experience. When we realize that the life principle in everything is One Life Principle, then we are able to see how it is that the spontaneous will of the Universe manifested in the individual gives the individual the right of choice under the Law of the Universe, but not beyond that.

There is no individual attraction. All may have it. It only appears that some persons are far more attractive than others because all do not individualize this attraction equally. Our personality is not something which developed itself, but is the use that we make of the creativeness with which we are endowed. Man in being creative is really but a user. He does not put creativeness into the soil; he takes it out. He does not put energy into the waterfall; he takes it out. That is why he is called a "husbandman," which literally means a dispenser of Divine gifts.

We cannot create attraction; spiritual attraction *is*. We do not even create our own muscles; they are developed by use but the use merely develops that which already existed. We wake up to our attractiveness by a process of mental reasoning, and we consciously use that attraction to bring into the social orbit of our life people and things reciprocal to our thought. It is of the greatest importance that we shall come to understand this. In spiritual mind treatment, if a practitioner thinks he has to create a Life Force by his thought, he is wasting time. If, on the other hand, he knows that the creative Force is, and his thought merely differentiates It, he practices scientifically and effectively.

You and I did not make this universal Creativeness. Emerson recognized this when he said: "From within or from behind, a light shines through us upon things, and makes us aware that we are nothing, but the light is all." And Jesus had no superstition about it. He said: " . . . the Father that dwelleth in me, he doeth the works." He believed that God was in him and he was in God and the two were one. That is what we must believe. Therefore, the creativeness behind our personality is the thing upon which we draw, the development of which is not its creation but its use of something greater than it is.

Anyone who has thought himself unattractive has undoubtedly prayed many times that God would show him what to do that men might like him and women praise him. He might be compared to a man standing knee-deep in a brook of clear fresh water and begging someone to give him a drink. His only need is to bend his head and drink to his heart's content. He needs only to open up the avenues of his mind, by a recognition of his oneness with eternal Beauty, and every attribute of good will manifest in his life for all to see. His attractiveness will cry from the housetops.

The Creativeness of the Universe is equally distributed among all people. It is the will of God. When I say "the will of God" I mean the nature of Being, because that is the will of God. God cannot will anything other than His own nature, and the will of God is the spontaneous nature of God everywhere. Therefore, the will of God is for the creativeness of man—the manifestation of the Divine in what we call the human—and that will cannot be more for one person than another. But biologically and psychologically people are by no means equal. I have to admit that some men are congenitally unfitted for certain tasks. I would not be so foolish as to think that everyone is intelligent enough to sit in the White House. But I am speaking of generic man, the universal Idea of which each one of us is a unique individualization.

Fortunately, we know now that it is not necessary that each of us shall be biologically and psychologically exactly alike, or what we call equal. There are people very much farther advanced than we are; there are others much less advanced, and my belief is that this goes on to infinity. I believe in the natural order of an evolving universe, visible and invisible, an infinite manifestation and an ever-evolving one, out of a potential which is an equal possibility to all people.

Someone may say that because we are not all alike we are not all perfect. Not at all. I believe in the natural, instinctive, spiritual, unconditioned and unviolated perfection of every living soul, no matter what he appears to be. But all are not evolved to the same point in the recognition of their perfection. Emerson said: "We wake and find ourselves on a stair: there are stairs below us, which we seem to have ascended; there are stairs above us, many a one, which go upward and out of sight." All great minds have perceived this same truth. Any man, whether he is sweeping streets, building bridges, preaching sermons, raising the dead, or running a hospital, that man— if he is fulfilling himself to the level of his present comprehension—is just as perfect as God. We will never get anywhere with a consistent spiritual philospohy unless we come to see that.

The only way we can ever use spiritual Power is by a conscious sense of unity. There is One Creativeness in the universe. We did not put It there and God Himself did not put It there. It *is* God, and God did not make God. It is individualized in each one of us. The way we use It manifests as our personality—our charm, our attractiveness—the visible evidence of our invisible subjective individualization of this universal Creativeness, acting as Law and Order. Therefore, when we are attuned to that inner Creativeness, we are consciously communicating with God. But according to our nature and Its nature, the truth of which is constructive, the destructive use of It automatically inhibits our evolution, automatically punishes us until we change our program and use It constructively. Consequently, our freedom is so great that we can abuse it, but not for long.

Psychology has been unable to satisfactorily explain to us what a person is, yet there is a known personalness. But we make a terrible mistake if we think the effect is its own cause. God is universal Intelligence—the infinite capacity to know and to be. It is impossible for the finite to grasp the full meaning of God. This infinite Being has within Itself what we may call an infinite Personalness. This does not mean that God is a person, as we think of a person. On the other hand, it does not limit the idea of Infinity to think that the Spirit has the elements of personalness.

You and I are persons; therefore there must be a universal Person manifesting Himself at the level of our perception. They accused Jesus of blasphemy because he understood that some day all people must come to know that the deep reservoir of their own minds is the eternal Mind, God, the living Spirit Almighty; and the creativeness of the mind of the individual existed in the Infinite eons before he ever used it.

One thing more we must not forget: When all the charm, all the beauty, all the attractiveness, which must be the Infinite, is loosed and spilled over man, the finite, only as much as the finite embodies can it experience, no more. Only as much as we bring into the kingdom of heaven can respond to us. May we, then, not feel justified in believing that this infinite Something which we call God, this universal Mind and Presence, is at this moment flowing in us and is us? Are we not infinite Attractiveness right this minute? In such degree as we embody It, automatically It embodies us.

# 7

# AS YOU BELIEVE

Ignorance and superstition have always been allies—"vultures of the same egg." And it is not surprising to find, in a country where for so many years there have been just two kinds of people, good and bad, there are yet individuals here and there puzzled about "goodness." Finally it reaches, through some insidious suggestion too subtle for understanding, the absurd height of asking: "Am I good enough to attempt to express more good?"

Because we have not reached the top, shall we refuse to take the first step? Because we have not prepared for calculus, shall we refuse to do our sums in addition? If the requirements followed these lines there would be no progress. Jesus refused to allow his disciples to call him good, explaining that there were none good except the Father. Shall we wait until we see as clearly as he saw the unity of all life before we attempt to use what light we have? Shall we bury our one talent and foolishly expect that we shall later dig it up and find it has multiplied into ten? Jesus said: " . . . He that believeth on me, the works that I do shall he do also; and greater works than these shall he do; because I go unto my Father." Greater things than Jesus did! Does this mean that we have to be better than he was to do this. Did he say that perfection was the thing that was required? On the contrary, he made it plain that *belief* was the one essential factor. " . . . as thou hast believed, so be it done unto thee . . . ."

Jesus fed the hungry, healed the sick, and raised the dead. If we are to do better than this, our spiritual mind treatments —our demonstrations—will have to begin right where we are, with exactly the mental equipment we have today, whether we call this good or bad.

It gives us a new sense of human values to realize that all humanity is Divinity waking up to Itself through self-discovery and self-realization. All our study and concern with theories is only that we may prove and practice them. Practice, then, is the art and the act and the science—art because it is a thing of perfect harmony; act because it is an aggressive, conscious thing; and a science because it is subject to exact laws—of bringing our thought, consciously and subjectively, to absolutely believe, accept, and embody statements and declarations which affirm the great realization of spiritual perception as now present in fact, in experience.

We know that we are the sum total psychologically of every-thing that has gone before. Spiritually, we are the offspring, if we wish to put it that way, the manifestation or emanation of a universal Wholeness. This universal Wholeness is in us in a very true sense of the term because, as the originating principle of life we have God, or universal Spirit, out of which anything and everything was made. Therefore every man is truly born of God. If this is true, then man is primarily and fundamentally perfect, no matter what he has done to himself.

But many people question: Am I good enough to try to bring out this realization in my life and the lives of others?

If by goodness is meant that state of being which some people think they attain by sacrifice and long suffering, such goodness has nothing to do with spiritual healing. We should not refuse to claim the greatest blessing that is ours merely for the accepting, just because we have thought we were not good enough. Is it not more likely that we are afraid someone who knows us will not think we are good enough? Are we not more afraid of what people think about us than what we think about ourselves? There is always something within man which constantly proclaims to him his Divinity, and which is always pushing out for expression, but we are stopped when we remember that those who know us might not believe we were sufficiently qualified. Let us banish from our thought the idea that the world must call us holy, as the world understands the word, before we can claim our wholeness with Good and demonstrate it for ourselves and others.

In spiritual healing one frees one's mind from self-condemnation. He knows to a certainty that there is no sin but a mistake and no punishment but a consequence, and that therefore there is nothing that can prevent him from healing spiritually at such time as he shall recognize his true relationship. But once he has taken this step, the only way he can successfully practice is to see nothing but perfection—perfect God, perfect Man, perfect Universe. However, it must be distinctly understood that spiritual healing does not create a perfect idea or a perfect body. It is revealing an idea which is already perfect.

Spiritual mind healing is not just psychological healing. It is different from the ordinary concept of prayer. It is not will power; it is not holding thoughts; it is not beseeching God to be God—God is already God. It is the actual determination on the part of the individual to intelligently, with as much emotion or feeling as possible, realize his own inherent, eternal, and never-changing being. Spiritual mind healing, in its highest sense, cannot be divorced from a true religious conviction. It is knowing the truth that the same pure Intelligence which is the volition and will of the Universe, is incarnated in us right now. The spiritual treatment becomes a statement of our belief, an affirmation of our investigation; and the ideas embodied in the treatment externalize in exact mathematical ratio as the beliefs which deny them are dissolved from our consciousness.

Besides the infinite Presence there is also an immutable Law which governs everything. Wherever we look we see Law in force. Not only are we to consciously draw inspiration from the Divine Presence, but we are consciously to use the Divine Law, combining what is called the personal and the impersonal elements into one unity.

We then say what we would like the Principle of Life to do for us. We do not wish a good for ourselves that would not be good for another. That is why Emerson said: "Prayer that craves a particular commodity,—any thing less than all good, —is vicious." But good is right; good cannot do evil. Abundance cannot hurt anybody. We should work consistently and definitely to convince ourselves that we are happy, surrounded by an environment of goodness and truth and beauty, of friendship, of everything that makes life worthwhile. It is not going to hurt the rest of the world for you and me to have plenty. It is not going to hurt the rest of the world for you and me to be happy. We are not trying to make the people around us think as we think. We do not have to watch the other person. There is nothing in the universe to watch but ourselves. We will never see or experience anything but ourselves.

No matter how inclusive our spiritual treatments may be as to the omnipresence of good for all persons, when we are giving treatments we must be very specific. If we wish to demonstrate a companion or a position, we are not treating to heal some physical ailment. If someone asks us how to get to a certain place, geographically, we do not direct him in the òpposite direction. Why, then, should we be chaotic in giving treatments? There is nothing more specific than spiritual mind treatment.

We must realize not only that with God all things are possible, but that poverty, disease, and other human ills do not have stages of development in Divine Mind. When doubts, fears, and contradictions come up in mind, we must turn to them and consciously and definitely put them out. We must remember that a thought is a thing. A thought that doubts good neutralizes a thought that affirms good, and vice versa. It does not matter what has happened or what condition exists, we must realize that we are using a Power compared to which the united intelligence of the human race is as nothing. We must continually affirm, with an ever-growing conviction, the active presence of good in our experience right now.

A treatment becomes a mental entity in the spiritual world, just as a kernel of corn becomes a physical entity in the creative force of nature which we call the soil, in conjunction with the elements. The word which we speak is complete and sure and has means and processes of producing itself at the level of our recognition. Consequently, as the recognition becomes greater, the experience becomes broader. We are dealing with absolute, unconditioned Causation right now, and in such degree as our concept embraces this conviction, we are able to demonstrate the condition we desire.

The sooner we realize that this is the truth about spiritual mind practice, the quicker we will demonstrate. This is the most marvelous thing in the world; it is the greatest discovery that was ever made by the mind of man. It taps the greatest resourcefulness that has ever been tapped, and it is absolutely real, whether or not we believe it. The first thing is to believe it. There is no approach without belief.

A spiritual mind treatment, for ourselves or another, is a conscious, moving, active thing, the conscious approach that we make to First Cause. We start with absolute Intelligence as fundamental. Just as I know that I exist and I respond to that thought, and you respond to me and I to you because of our intelligence, Intelligence must recognize and respond to Itself. The only way Intelligence can respond to Itself is by corresponding with Itself. So our approach to First Cause is mental, because it is a thing of consciousness. It should be scientific, because it is built upon the theory that we are surrounded by a universal Law which accepts our thought and acts creatively upon it. It should also be a thing of faith. We should have the same faith in a spiritual mind treatment that we have that nature will invariably act in accord with harmonious laws—an acceptance and belief equal to that built upon an understanding that if we put certain combinations of natural forces together, they will produce certain other combinations. Just the same faith that we have that when we plant potatoes, we shall later dig potatoes and not turnips.

All we have to do is to place our request, believe it, and let it alone. The hardest thing any man has to do is to learn to trust the Universe. It would seem that it might be the easiest thing to do, but it is not. We like to dabble with our request; pull our prayer back; give our treatment and then steal back to see if it is taking root. We might excuse a child if we found him digging up a seed two days after planting to see if it were growing. But we, as adults, should be wiser than to plant our thought seed one day and dig it up the next.

An individual giving a treatment must believe that there is

a Power that responds to his thought. No matter what all the world believes, no matter what anyone says, he must believe that this Power does, directly and specifically, respond to his word; that he is actually in league with the only Power there is. Without this conviction, our word returns unto us void.

We are to approach the Presence simply, directly, and easily, because It is right here within us. We can never get outside ourselves. We shall always be interior in our comprehension. Consequently, the one wishing to demonstrate must turn to his own mind and his own thought, because in his own mind and his own thought is the place where he is an individualized center of God-consciousness.

We put into a treatment what we desire to come out of it. Many people may take this to mean that we must inject a positive force and energy into a reluctant force of nature and compel it to work. This is not so at all. If we put corn into the ground, we get corn, but we do not have to make the corn come out of the soil. We could not do so. If we had to put into our thought the force to make that thought creative, we would be lost.

A potential possibility remains latent until the mind acts upon it. What would it benefit us if the potentiality of the Universe lay at our feet and we didn't use it? As soon as we comply with any law of nature it immediately is known to us, but until it is known to us it is just exactly as though it had no existence. In the evolution of his thought man provides avenues through which potentialities come into being. Man does not create anything except the form, the shape, and the use. Electricity might have been used centuries ago if man had created an avenue for it.

Anyone can effectively heal spiritually who believes that he can and will take the time to put that belief into motion through the Law. If we are troubled by an imaginary hindrance—the thought that we must attain a degree of perfection before we dare use any of the knowledge we have about God—we should build up our faith by a realization of what we are: One with the Infinite. We should conceive of all good—health, happiness, and abundance—existing for us and for all men. We should remember that *belief* is the power which sustains thought in its creative activity in Mind, and it must be uncolored by any meagerness or mediocrity of past experience.

When we have strengthened our belief by aligning ourselves with the nature of Reality, which is wholeness and unity, goodness, truth, and beauty, we shall see that we do not have to contend with anything on earth. We do not have to struggle to find a place for ourselves. In the sight of the Almighty—which is in the sight of our own spiritual natures—we are of It, no matter where we are.

*8*

# THE CHOICE IS YOURS

It is not inconceivable that a few generations from now, when a little leaven shall have leavened the whole, historians may record this age as the period of man's great stupidity. It is understandable even now. If we were notified tomorrow that a deceased relative had left us a million dollars and we had only to identify ourselves and receive the fortune, what would be our reaction? Many of us would mentally claim the money and begin spending it before the check was in our hands. Others would conservatively await the receipt of the check before changing the basis of their living. But what of the man who paid no attention to it, the man who treated it as he might treat a notice that he had won a shaving mug? Probably the kindest thought any of us would have about him would be that that man should certainly have a guardian.

Yet thousands of us are just as crassly foolish. In the midst of the greatest abundance the world has ever seen we suffer because of lack. We remain enmeshed in the throes of poverty when we could have riches inexhaustible. We choose blindness when we could have vision. We accept the portion of sorrow which negative thinking lays in our lap when joy is our inheritance. We live in turmoil when we might have peace.

We are like a sculptor having both the training and the

tools with which to work, standing before a huge block of marble, admiring its beauty yet never turning a hand, and all the while wondering why an interesting statue does not emerge —entirely forgetful of why he had studied for years and why he has tools with which to work. We are like a man who hates darkness and sits alone in a house completely wired for electricity, praying for the light yet never moving a finger to switch on the powerful illumination. Will it be strange if future generations, knowing all this, call us stupid?

How many people in the world really believe that all good is theirs right now? Not one in a thousand. Too long we have formed the habit of thinking a thing "too good to be true." Nothing is too good to be true. If a man feels consciously or subjectively unable to cope with life, it is because he does not understand that every individual is a unique individualization of the Universe Itself; that there is something in him that is primordial, perfect, complete, and all he needs to do is to develop that and not fall prostrate at the feet of those people whom his mistaken viewpoint thinks must be great. Emerson said that the greatness that men have, we have given them. We drape greatness about them from our own perception.

It is the Father's good pleasure to give us the kingdom, therefore there can be no failure in the giving. We must know that. The kingdom is already given us. Abundance is already given us. And freedom is already given us.

Everything is created on an infinite and limitless design, because it rests on an infinite, limitless basis, and the whole order of evolution is to produce individualized freedom, still acting as a perfect unity. God, being Himself freedom, could not create man and at the same time not create a way in which man could be as free as God, because it is only out of God's freedom that He can make anything. Whether we form the belief emotionally, religiously, or intellectually, we are bound to arrive at the conclusion that in making man God had to make a way whereby man would automatically be free. Let us recognize and rejoice in this freedom. The more completely we plumb the human mind, the more it ought to yield. Instead of its being exhausted by use, it grows by use. There is that which increaseth as it scattereth. We are dealing with an infinite and final Unity, which, though It appears to break down into multiplicity, never breaks down Its unity.

We might as well proceed from this viewpoint: We are this moment in an infinite Mind which presses against us, is in us, and is our mind. It is not only Its own Mind, but It is also our mind, because we are made out of It, and there is nothing out of which It could make us but Itself. We are in infinite Mind and infinite Mind is in us. It is by this Mind that we think. This Mind is eternal; therefore we are eternal. This Mind is complete; therefore we are complete. This Mind is substance; therefore we are one in essence with all the substance of the universe.

We do not appear complete. We act as if we were temporal, limited, unprepared, and afraid. We are not so foolish as to think that people do not suffer; that they do not experience want; that they are not unhappy. But the potential I, the potential you, is just as perfect as the inherent God. This is why the world will call us stupid: that we do not call this perfection into objective manifestation. It is not a matter of choice that we are potentially perfect. It is not a matter of conjecture. If we wish we might say it is the gift of God. As Jesus said: "Fear not, little flock; for it is your Father's good pleasure to give you the kingdom." Goodness is already given. We may have misinterpreted it; we may have used our very freedom to bind ourselves. In fact, I think we do that very thing and the intelligence which we use in the wrong way is the only thing that can make us unhappy.

Someone might argue that faith and fear are entirely different attitudes. Really fear is nothing more than misplaced faith—faith in a power opposed to good. I believe it is all one and every experience we have is as real as it is supposed to be. It is not necessary to deny objective reality, not necessary to deny that we suffer or that we are unhappy, in order to understand Reality, and no great thinker has ever done so. Goodness is already given, the Divine Gift is made, and as we awake to the realization of It, It is ours. That is what spiritual demonstration is.

We shall find everything that we believe is perfectly logical and inevitably necessary, fundamentally so; but it is the misconception of the way that it works that causes confusion in the individual mind. A spiritual mind treatment is a rational thing, but it is a thing of feeling too. What are we doing when we make our demand? We are invoking the Law on our behalf, that It shall do a certain specific thing for us, but we are not limiting the way the thing shall be done. The only man who can know whether or not this is so, is the man who can prove it, and he will know it to the extent that he does prove it. It is there to be used. It has been proved by many. The discouraging thought that it may not be good for us to have a greater good should never enter our mind. We are certainly not going to be able to experience a greater good while we deny its existence. We cannot realize the good we desire as long as we say, "I know I cannot get it because I have no pull." Our progress does not depend on the influence or even the goodwill of any man. It is not "pull" we need, but to listen more intently to the inner *push* of the Spirit, which is forever pressing against us for expression.

The trouble is that for so long the world has looked upon things spiritual as being unnatural that men stand a little aghast at the word. And they are practically incredulous when told that by their own thought they can reach out and contact the Source of all Good; by their own thought they can demonstrate abundance; by their own thought they can change joy into sorrow; by their own thought they can change their physical environment. It at first sounds so incredible that thousands of us never even try it. But when the time shall come that we can speak of spiritual things normally and naturally, when we can get together and talk about our spiritual experiences and no longer feel that such talk is weird or queer, then we shall have removed one of the big stumbling blocks to our growth.

The soul feels it is united with the whole, but we have to consciously sense the union, individually. Consequently, people with an adequate spiritual conviction are in a better state of health than those who do not have a spiritual conviction. The person who wishes a healing must understand something about Spirit. He may do it in a crude way or a refined way, but he must do something to get the conviction into his consciousness that he does not walk alone in life; that there is a Presence and a Power inherent within him which is greater than anything he shall ever contact. Then it shall be that his life will be a constant unfoldment in grace, charm, enthusiasm, and a great sense of peace.

Everything is all right, right this minute, if we only knew it. This is true and at the same time it is not true. It is true in principle, so far as Reality is concerned. Nothing more will ever be provided for our good than has already been provided. But that which is true in principle is only as true in practice as we make it. Though we are surrounded by beauty, for instance, only as much enters our consciousness as we allow to enter, only as much as we can appreciate. Even though this All-Good is ever-available and immediately responsive, we have a part to play in bringing this into our experience. The fortune was willed the man, but since he would not cash the check it was as though it never belonged to him.

Above all things we must know definitely and consistently that the Universe is for us and not against us. But someone will say: "It is not true that the Universe is for us. Look at the evil, the lack, the limitation, the physical pain and anguish of the human race." Particularly will people say, as many have believed for countless years, that God *wants* them to suffer. Such a thought is perfect nonsense. We must convince our mind that God does not, could not, desire evil. We shall also have to get over the agelong determination to believe that evil is an entity. We shall have to learn that evil is not person, place, nor thing, but is an experience we are allowed to have because of our Divine individuality, until through negative experiences we learn to use the Law affirmatively, to cooperate with It and thus enjoy Its full benefits. For the true Law is a Law of liberty and not of bondage. Our sins were forgiven us before we ever sinned, which, however, does not mean that we can keep on sinning and get away with it. The Universe is foolproof. It does say that we can have what we want, but It also says that we shall have to take into our experience the logical result of our thinking, be it good or what we call evil. The Law is as impersonal as electricity. It will warm us or burn us, according to the way we use It.

We want to use the Law of Mind to demonstrate our good. If it be that we can be well, if we can be happy, if we can be prosperous, if we can have a fuller life by our thinking, then we should like to begin. How shall we go about it? First, our spiritual mind treatments must be based on the proposition that the Universe is limitless and immediately responds to us. Even if we do not know a person of influence to give us a helping hand, Spirit fills every place so every place is a place of influence. In a spiritual mind treatment for the betterment of conditions we must first be sure that what we want is in unity with Good, and then the gaining of our desire can only produce good to ourselves and to everyone else. We must believe that the Universe Itself desires us to have this good because in our expressing this good It is expressing Itself. We must have faith that the Law instantly responds to us, and we must understand that for every action there is an equal reaction, which means that at the level of our recognition will it be done.

A spiritual mind treatment is a reaction of the mind upon itself, entirely. Someone may say that it is a reaction of the mind upon the Universe. The treatment itself must be a reaction of the mind upon itself. There is only one Self. In such degree, then, as the mind perceives, understands, and mentally and spiritually assimilates perfection, the result of the treatment will be perfect. The reaction is equal to the belief. Therefore, our word should be spoken in belief, in conviction, in complete and implicit trust, and, above all else, our word should not be limited by any existing circumstances. The word creates its own mathematics; it creates its own outlet. The demand that the word makes upon the Universe creates the way for the demand to be met. This is in line with the later idea of evolution among the great thinkers of the world: that when the mind needs anything with which to more fully express itself, the thing arises out of the demand.

When we think of Spirit as being fluidic, waiting to flow into the form which our thought directs, we shall be able to lose sight of objective conditions. If we say, "But I have no money with which to pay the rent. I don't know which way to turn," and our thought is engrossed with our lack, does that not constitute our belief? Is not that our treatment? Not only is it a treatment, but it will demonstrate just as it is given: We will have no money with which to pay the rent; we will not know which way to turn.

Something is radically wrong with the manner in which men have tried to solve their problems without taking God into consideration. There has been too much misery and unhappiness. It seems we would welcome the information that help is at hand. Shouldn't it bring tremendous happiness when we learn that there is a Divine Law upon which happiness and prosperity depend? Is it not cause for rejoicing when we learn that we can consciously unite with the Source of our good? With the knowledge of these tools which are at hand we know how to work. Whenever any thought arises within us which denies us the right to demonstrate a more abundant good, we may know that thought arises out of the psychological nature of our experience and our reaction to it. It does not arise as a pure image of the Spirit, which can conceive only freedom and knows only good, understands only peace, and lives only in the consciousness of self-expression. Spiritual mind treatment is effective only in such degree as we get back to the conviction that we are dealing with a Power that makes and remakes. So, as these unpleasant objective conditions are brought into our mind, we say to ourselves that they are like a picture which is cast on a screen, and it is our business to get back of the picture to the mind which projected it and change the picture.

To say it all in a little different way: From the standpoint of the spiritual Universe there is no solid fact; there is merely outlined form. The findings of modern science tend to affirm this position. The material universe is not a thing in itself, but it has a definite meaning; its business is to give form to Spirit. The human body is some part of this form. If we can accept this position as true, we can come to believe that the nature of the Spirit is to control the flow of the form. Then we can understand how it was that Jesus was able to heal the para- lyzed man and to say to the blind man: "See!" Jesus did not create the ability of the man to reach out and grasp at a physical object; he merely recreated the idea of the instrument which could reach out. He did not create vision; he remolded the concept of vision. In such degree as we understand this principle we shall be able to perform the same so-called miracles, and it will be in accord with Law. But we must first come to sense the spiritual Universe as real and know that the power of our word, in conjunction with the Spirit, is immutable. We should learn to transpose the physical universe for a spiritual one and call upon the invisible side of ourselves. This is far more than suggestion; it is the realization of Life. The Essence of Life is ever-present. The intellectual and mental faculties mold this Essence into form; conviction measures It out.

We must believe. " . . . they . . . entered not in because of unbelief." We must not limit the Infinite. And we can begin right now to heal ourselves of physical troubles, of mental fears, of lack and limitation. When enough people can believe that by pure reason, or by perfect faith, spiritual healing of the body can follow, then everyone will naturally seek that method. It is not going to do us any good to wait until the world comes out of its confusion. It is not going to do the world any good for us to sit down and cry with it. Jesus said: "And I, if I be lifted up from the earth, will draw all men unto me." He did not say "if I be dragged down." So each one of us must be continuously endeavoring to promote his own welfare, not at the expense of someone else, but by applying the principle directly and immediately to himself, for himself, in himself.

But suppose you will not accept your good, should I deny myself the privilege of experiencing my good? If I refuse to be at peace in my own consciousness, is it then necessary that you, too, shall refuse to be at peace in your consciousness in order that you might show that you sympathize with me? Not at all. " . . . Can the blind lead the blind? shall they not both fall into the ditch?"

It is only when we see clearly to walk ourselves that we are able to choose a direction which another will desire to take. I think each one of us is beholden to himself, and to the world, to live a normal, well-balanced, fruitful life, demonstrating to the fullest his ability, love, and self-expression. The Infinite has enough for all, so it is not selfish to demonstrate happiness, joy, harmony, peace, beauty, love, friendship, and right action. They already exist and we must use them. Individually, we must look for the best, expect the best, and know that the best is going to come, and so reduce the number that future generations shall call stupid because their good was at hand and they failed to use it.

9

# THE POWER OF PRAYER

Most people who believe in God, believe in prayer. We are all more or less familiar with different religious beliefs and approaches to Reality, each prescribing a way to pray. And each way is right for him who believes in it. I believe that every man's prayer is good, but I believe that all men's prayers, insofar as they are effective, are effective because they embody certain universal principles, which, if we understood them, we could consciously use, and that power which is obtained by a few would be as easily used by all.

The Bible promises: "If ye abide in me, and my words abide in you, ye shall ask what ye will, and it shall be done unto you." "Abide in" carries with it not only the thought of continuous existence in, but a thought of permeation, oneness *with*—a oneness with God wherein man may ask what he will and it will be given him. When man recognizes his oneness with Good, what can he ever ask aside from good for all men?

To say that there are, or may be, certain things for which we are prohibited from praying may sound paradoxical to those who have not analyzed what prayer is. But if we are abiding in Him we shall not be able to think upon or recognize evil or adversity, either for ourselves or for any man. Granting that *we* could know it, it would not be possible for God to know it,

71

and it would be impossible to talk to Him about something of which He was unaware. And He can only know Perfection. Therefore we cannot pray for evil or misfortune to come upon any man.

Obviously, if we pray for understanding, for joy, for peace, for love, for prosperity, for any *good* thing, He will give it to us. It will not be a matter of overcoming God's reluctance, it will instead be a matter of our acceptance of His highest willingness. This brings to our mind again the fact that no law is set in motion to answer our prayer; we simply recognize a Law that has always existed and put ourselves in alignment with It. Emerson said: "Is not prayer also a study of truth, a sally of the soul into the unfound infinite?"

Prayer is essential, not to the salvation of the soul for the soul is never lost, but to the conscious well-being of the soul which does not understand itself. There is a vitality in man's relationship to the Infinite which is productive of more good than any other vitality man has ever encountered in the journey of his evolution. As fire warms our bodies, as food strengthens us and sunshine raises our spirits, so there is a subtle transfusion of some invisible force as we pray, weaving itself into the warp and woof of our own mentalities.

If spiritual things be true, it is not enough simply to declare they are so. We have to understand how they work and why—the laws governing them. Then we shall be able to say: Here it is; this is the way it works. You can use it and I can use it. There is no special dispensation of Providence; there is no God who cares more for the Jews than He does for the Gentiles, or cares more for the Gentiles than He does for the Jews. As intelligent observers we must realize that God is a universal Presence, a divine and impartial Giver, forever pouring Himself upon His creation.

If we wish to be beneficiaries of this Divine influx we must consciously receive it. Many people imagine that one man has a secret about God that some other man does not have. I do not believe there is anyone living who has been given the secret to the kingdom of heaven. No one man knows the one and only way of salvation. If we put together all the knowledge that the world has about chemistry and related subjects, all that the scientists have been able to determine about it, then we have the science of chemistry. If we arrange in proper order all the findings of all the psychologists of the world, we have the science of psychology. And our position is that if we will collect the teachings of the spiritual geniuses of all ages and put the volumes into one group, we will be able to discover what the world knows about the science of Spirit. Therefore, it is necessary to break down the boundary lines of isolated opinions and come into the broader field and greater perspective.

We say, in our system of thought, that there is nothing but God, and that when we talk to each other God is communicating Himself to Himself. It is small wonder that people who believe that Divinity is an external thing should think we are sacrilegious. But if that Something which we call God, in Its essence and in our approach to It, is not to be found in our own spirit then we shall never find It. Emerson said: "He [man] must greatly listen to himself." And Jesus said: " . . . he that hath seen me hath seen the Father . . . ." God must be, and is, a universal Essence, an undivided and indivisible Spirit, omnipresent, and present in our own spirit as that which we are at this moment. Our approach to this Divine creative Principle is the Still Small Voice. God is an indwelling Presence. I do not believe in lost souls, but I do believe that every living soul is in search of himself and his relationship to whatever

Reality is. We have come to believe there is a Reality which we sense in our own being, giving birth to a direct relationship to the Infinite—all the magnificence and the beauty and the power and the peace which is commensurate with the estimation of the meaning of the Infinite, God.

Mind must be the thing that prays. We cannot arrive at any other conclusion. Without mind there is no philosophy, there is no science, there is no psychology, there is no religion. There is no prayer and no answer and no Universe unless there is a mind to be aware of it. What is mind? No one knows what mind is. No one knows what matter is. Theoretically, we dissolve it but it is still there—a material object, or lines of force in energy. There is no one living who knows what it is, and yet if a man denied it was there we would say he was insane. All we know about mind is that mind is that thing in me, whatever it is, which enables me to know that I am. It is that in you which enables you to know that you are. If I had a mind which was all mine, and you had one which was all yours, how could you know that I exist or how could I talk to you? Therefore we believe that there is only One Mind in the universe and It is incarnated in every one of us.

God must be universal Mind. God must be the power by which we think, will, and know. Therefore it follows that prayer to God is a communication with that inner Life, with that Divine indwelling Spirit, which is everywhere present, omnipotent and all-powerful. Jesus taught his disciples to pray: "Our Father which art in heaven, Hallowed be thy name." If you study that prayer you will find it is a straight affirmation of the presence of God, the Parent Mind, in man, for he had already said: "The kingdom of God is within you."

"But thou, when thou prayest, enter into thy closet [into your own mind] and when thou hast shut thy door [shut out objective struggle], pray to thy Father which is in secret; and thy Father which seeth in secret shall reward thee openly." That means the invisible Cause of life is contacted by the mind; the invisible Cause is set in motion by this act of the mind, and the objectification takes place following this interior process. That is what prayer is. If we think God is a distant Presence, a heavenly Dictator—something apart from that which lives and moves and has its being right where we are—then we are certain to believe ourselves disconnected from this infinite Being. But if we think of God as an indwelling Presence, our form of prayer is naturally addressed to a Presence in us that shall tend to awaken our own mind to It.

Someone might say: Where does God come in in this performance? God does not *come in*. God never went out. Every word we speak is God, everything we see is God—the buttercup, the sunset, the morning dew nestling in the petal of the rose, that is God, and love and laughter are God. God is everything, everywhere, every place—the innermost presence of our own thought, the outermost rim and circumference of our own experience.

It is not a burnt offering the Infinite requires, but a clean mind, a pure heart, an honest and sincere purpose, a direct belief, and a complete acceptance. Thus Solomon prayed for greater wisdom, for a more nearly Divine understanding. And Jesus prayed that all people should see what he saw, that they might be "in me and I in thee." We believe in prayer, but we call it something else. We call it spiritual mind treatment, which is the conscious act, through meditation and contemplation, of definitely accepting the presence of a good which the objective world cannot see, back of which is the belief that we are surrounded by a Creativeness or Law which intelligently responds to us. It is not a beseechment, because it rests upon the belief that the Universe already desires to do this, and must, because that is Its nature. Therefore, what we do in a spiritual mind treatment is to align the mind, the thought, with form, which is the manifestation of that Spirit. The physical universe is a mold and nothing else; it is an effect, never a cause.

The first step in affirmative prayer, or spiritual mind treatment, is the recognition of this universal creative Presence and Power which surrounds us and is responsive to us. Then the next step is meditation or unification with this Presence. Prayer has stimulated countless millions of people to nobler deeds and nobler thoughts, because anything that tends to connect our minds with this Over-Soul of the Universe lets in a flood of Its consciousness. The prayers of Jesus were an acceptance, a realization rather than request. No other man has ever lived who so continuously recognized, accepted, and practiced the Presence of God. Whatever the enlightenment of this man's mind was, it certainly placed him in a relationship to the infinite Being we call God which was so close, so immediate, that it was more like two people talking with each other. Jesus came preaching a gospel of fulfillment here and now for everybody. He did not try to tell God the better way to do things.

Recognition, unification (or meditation), and realization (or acceptance) are all mental acts, something which the mind does to itself. Meditation is a conscious attempt to establish in one's mind the recognition that a unity exists between man and God. Then one no longer says: "God, please give me a crust of bread, I am starving." That is a prayer of limitation, a denial of the abundance of the universe. That deifies want and crystalizes impoverishment. Meditation is the conscious act of definitely unifying the mind with the Spirit. Jesus said: "I and my Father are one." Our meditations are prayers put in the form of affirmations—the conscious association of unity, a belief in the inevitability of unity, and the desire to mentally accept that unity.

The last step, and perhaps the greatest, is acceptance or realization, the entering into the essence of that good which is desired in one's own life. It is the highest act that the human mind can reach because it no longer merely meditates on good, but itself becomes the good which was the object of its meditation. Then it is that the soul itself, as Emerson said, is nimble and hops about. It beholds its own glory everywhere. The individual no longer feels that the thing is *going* to be, or *ought* to be, or *must* be, but he knows that it *is* and he enters into it and it enters into him. Good is no longer a thing apart from the soul; Truth is not something to be attained; God is no longer something toward which we aspire; and the soul, alone and naked and unafraid, merges into the Universe, not to the loss of its individuality, but to the glorification of it.

With this understanding of the complete process and purpose of prayer or meditation, we are reminded of the many things we had meant to pray for, the variety of things we had thought we wanted that automatically fall away. Among the things we cannot pray for are fame and inordinate ambition. Such ambition as is born of the desire to completely express our individuality is a praiseworthy undertaking. It might easily come under the head of "the hunger and thirst after righteousness." But inordinate ambition, that which will elevate one man above his fellowmen, we cannot pray for. Nor for fame. Both are misnomers based on the supposition that one man be greater than another. This is impossible, for all men are Sons of God. No prestige could be greater, and no man can have less.

We cannot pray for our good to come to us through particular channels and at the same time expect that it will be a perfect demonstration. That would be based on the supposition that God is limited and could only fill our need through one channel. We might be greatly limiting that infinite Supply which is already rushing toward us. And we cannot pray to go to heaven. We are in heaven now. The kingdom of heaven is within us. No condition, no place, no person except oneself can cheat one out of the kingdom of heaven. It is a state of mind. Furthermore, we cannot pray for anything for ourselves, the coming of which would cheat or in any manner hurt another, for no thought like that can penetrate the consciousness of one *abiding* in Him. We can only ask for good, for Good is the nature of God.

The approach to God must be spontaneous. We need not worry about salvation. God is for us. But if we seek to destroy, we will be destroyed; and when we are tired of being destroyed we will stop it and nothing will have happened to the soul itself. Frequently our eyes are so veiled with the tears of anguish that we fail to see the glories around us; our ears so filled with discord that we are unable to hear the music of the spheres; and our thought, unattuned to Divine inspiration, is choked with the morbid reactions of life, the unhealthful reactions, the little bickering petty-isms of life. Would it not be wonderful if we could learn to expand and let the soul grow in beauty and joy?

Whenever prayer becomes meditation and meditation becomes transmuted into acceptance, there is always a demonstration. We can have what we want, but we have to take what goes with it. We all have the same potential power Jesus had, and our work should exist for the purpose of stimulating the realization so that we will know that we can know. Nothing brings such a consciousness of completion to the mind of a man as the knowledge that there is a direct action in his own mind which, operating independently of any objective condition, can transcend it without confusion. The mind consciously enters the realm where things are made out of nothing that we see and where the word itself becomes flesh and dwells among us.

Every man is his own savior because every man has a direct approach to Reality. Let us learn to believe and to perceive and daily to announce our Oneness with God. And whenever negation comes up in our consciousness, let us declare the affirmative and *know* that there is One bearing witness with us, even the Spirit of God, that wherever there is light there is no darkness. Every man has the power of faith and understanding to remold and remake his life, to recreate his destiny, not by willing but by being willing to know. Not by coercion; the race is not to the fast but to the surefooted. The race is not to anyone who contends with any powers, visible or invisible, but to the one who knows. God is not afar off. "But the word is very nigh unto thee, in thy mouth, and in thy heart, that thou mayest do it."

Let us feel the direct, indwelling presence of a Power sufficient to meet every human need, and accept that It not only desires to, but that it is Its business to, when we live in unity with It. Living in unity with It is very simple—the act of acceptance, belief, acquiescence, and embodiment. Then will our Oneness with Spirit be so complete there can be no question as to what we may pray for.

# 10

# THINKING CREATIVELY

The world has lost faith in much that at one time was considered authority. When we lose faith in the authority of any existing institution we are very likely, in repudiating its tenets, to throw out something that we should have kept. We are not alarmed over the thought that we shall suffer greatly in the dropping of many creeds and ceremonies, but we are anxious that we shall hold on to God.

Some people become fanatical in trying to discover Truth. Let us try to keep perfectly sane in our pursuit, always recognizing that fanaticism is accompanied by personal egotism, and that personal egotism leads into fanaticism. There would be no religious fanaticism if man understood religion and its universality. There should be no danger of a sane man losing his reason in the pursuit of spiritual things, because all insanity is the result of a disconnection of the mind with Reality, with actuality, with everyday affairs. Therefore, in our spiritual awakening we do not need to separate ourselves. To do so is a mistake. The method of approach is to have a spiritual outlook wherever we are. It is by so unifying life with Reality that we may come to see in every objective symbol a spiritual cause and a reason for its being. There is a way to arrive at peace and happiness in what we are now doing.

Whether our problems are social or economic, the science of mind, rightly understood, is a valuable asset in the fine art of living. We have foolishly thought that we could insult the integrity of the Universe and prosper. But man is a spiritual expression, and as such must find his real satisfaction in the things that endure. We must awaken to the truth that essentially this world order in which we live is a spiritual order; that honesty, justice, and love are the very foundations of all life, and they cannot be flaunted with impunity, for they are the moral and spiritual principles that underlie all human relationships.

This inquiry into our problems is producing a rapid evolution in our thought. But the inquiring attitude is a healthy mental state. The world, spiritually speaking, is in better condition than it has been because out of all the controversy, the mental turmoil, there will come some kind of an answer. And the new answer must provide a bridge between the intellect and the emotions. It must be intelligent, scientific, and artistic.

It may be asked: What can we depend upon? Whom can we trust? The answer is: First set our mental and spiritual house in order and then, insofar as possible, make it produce for us the necessary and the beautiful things of life. What can be more practical than to gain the ability to demonstrate in our experience that we can consciously call on a higher Power to do our bidding, whenever our will is in conjunction with Its nature, with the full assurance that It can never withhold our real good from us.

Each one is seeking to reinterpret life to himself. There are certain things which we must know about ourselves, inside as well as outside. We may look about for saviors but we shall not find them. We may listen to sages, and can interpret or misinterpret what they say; but we will never find any satisfactory answer outside of an immediate, personal, spiritual experience, a certain interior awareness through which the soul recognizes itself as being in unity with the Universe and with all other selves. The most impossible mental state is one which does not know that good must come at last to each alike.

In attempting to analyze our mind we must realize that all that we can analyze is what the mind *does*. We assume certain things to be true of the mind because of what it does. What the mind itself is no one knows. In theorizing on what the mind appears to be we are conscious of the most striking fact: Mind is the one and only energy we know of in nature which is conscious of itself and, at the same time, conscious of other energies. Electricity is an energy and appears to be an intelligent one, but it is not at all probable that electricity is conscious of itself. The creative power in the soil is most certainly intelligent, multiplying and bringing forth exactly what is given to it, but it is not probable that it is conscious of what it is doing. However, while it is not conscious of what it is doing, it still brings to bear an Intelligence upon its acts, so much greater than our conscious intelligence that we cannot even compare the two. It is an interesting fact that our conscious mind, in our everyday walk of life, is dealing with creative intelligences in nature which do not know that they are creative intelligences, but which still know how to be what they are and know how to do what they do.

One thing is certain, the more deeply we penetrate the mind, instead of exhausting that which we are penetrating, the more we discover how much is to be penetrated. We might have so much water in a reservoir and when we have used it, it is gone; so much money in the bank and when we have drawn it out and spent it, it is gone; so much food in the larder and when we have eaten it, that is the end of it. Everything in the objective world begins and ends in the duration of time. But when we enter ourselves we discover ourselves to be an inexhaustible reservoir. Why is this unless there is really an inexhaustible Self which we all may sense and experience?

This great exploration which the mind makes into the realm of spiritual healing is as fascinating an experience as anyone will ever have. We must be careful, however, to differentiate between this form of thinking and mere daydreaming. In daydreaming one sits around longing for things, and picturing oneself as having them, but in the very same moment being certain it could never be, letting one's imagination run wild, soaring into realms of fancy. Some people have done this and upon being told that they had not proceeded properly, have exclaimed: "But we understood that we could have anything we wished." In spiritual mind practice a person does not just "wish" for things. He consciously uses his thought to set creative Power in motion and then accepts with expectancy the result. He is, in a certain sense, experimenting not with Mind Itself, but with his own thought, in seeing what use he can make of the creative Power of Mind. This Creativeness we do not inject into Mind; It is there already, a natural Law in the universe.

In spiritual treatment the person thinks of himself as he would like to be. He should do this without contradicting the good of others, without seeking to coerce others. And he should do this in as absolute sense as possible; that is, he should withdraw from any contemplation of the relative facts in the case and think only of the desired outcome as being established in Mind. He takes a proposition which his mind can encompass —such as realizing that he is surrounded by abundance and by right opportunity—and compels his mind to accept this idea as now being a fact in his everyday experience. Consequently,

his work is intensely practical, and even though he is an idealist
he is scientific in his application of this universal Principle of
Mind to the problems of his daily living.

Whether we think we are dealing with our individual minds
or with the universal Mind, we are dealing with the same
thing. What we call the individual mind is merely the place
where the individual uses the creative Power of Mind; man
expressing God at the level of his intelligence. And the beautiful part is that we do not have to tell Mind how to bring about
the thing we are demanding of It. Mind finds Its own avenue
and outlet, and releases Its own energies for the purpose of
self-expression.

The ever-availability of Good, through the use of our mind,
means added wisdom for anything and everything we under-
take. Every man can prove the proposition for himself and the
Almighty has already given him the power. We shall never
know that it actually works until we try it, but once we have
proved it there is added to our lives and our experiences a
something which will so change us that we shall never again
be the same; our whole reaction to life will forever be different.
We shall have made one definite step in the spiritual evolution
of the soul.

Often we say that we cannot see our way out of certain
conditions. We do not have to see our way *out*. We have to
know that there is a way *in* to that innermost region of us
which coexists with First Cause. Right now there is a Power
in you and in me which is God. There is a Presence which is
Good, an Intelligence which is Perfect. In this sacred spot of
the Most High within us we dwell quietly and calmly until we
reach a conviction that all is right with us. If we wait for it,
it will not come, but when we believe in it, it will be there.
It has nothing whatever to do with time.

We shall finally be delivered because the Universe is fool-proof, a Universe of law and order, of cause and effect, and nothing can be more wonderful than the majestic, sublime, and eternal march of cause and effect. Our part is to unify with the Universe by deliberately turning from discord to harmony, to the belief that in the spiritual world there is a counterpart, a prototype, a real entity back of us, though it is only partially and imperfectly revealed in our human way of thinking. Spiritual healing is the result of our attempt to seek out the universal Harmony, to unify ourselves with the Life of God.

It is superstitious to believe that Spirit cares more for one than another or that Truth is partial to any individual. It comes to all alike. The sun shines alike on the just and the unjust. Each in his own tongue interprets the God that is, and out of the God that is and must be creates the image of the God he worships. This has always been so and perhaps always will be. Enlightenment alone will create the image out of the God that really is.

As an instance of the practical value of this principle to any kind of business, let us take the example of a man who believes he is not a good salesman because he does not make friends. At any rate, he feels the need of friendship. This man is typical of countless individuals whose experiences have been such that they think everything is against them and nothing for them. No one loves them; no one considers them; no one plans for them.

If such a man is intelligent enough to recognize the absence of friends, he is intelligent enough to perceive the qualities which enter into friendship: loyalty, honesty, integrity, understanding, and such. The first step for him to take is to become friendly in his own thought. When he recognizes that he is joined to every other person by their common heritage of good, he can easily prepare for friendship by creating an atmosphere of love and harmony in his heart. Not anywhere else but in his own thought.

He might begin by saying to himself: "Everything is One. The Mind which I use, which I call my mind, is the same Mind that every other human being uses, so there can be no ill will or opposition in any man's mind toward me. I have no enemies. I am one with all Good. But every man is one with all Good; therefore, I am one with every man. Wherever I go, whenever I go, I am meeting friendship, love, kindness, and consideration. I am loving every man and am desiring every man's good as I desire my own. I give to every man kindness and unselfish service. Therefore, these have to come back to me in friendship, for universal Mind can deny me nothing." Whoever does this will find friends wherever he goes.

All men believe in God, but all men are not aware that they believe in God. The only way we shall ever know what God is to us is by an inner conviction, which will be theoretical, and an externalization of that, which will be practical. The inner conviction we have; and we wish now to externalize it. We align ourselves in principle with God, who is our Creator, the Essence of the thing desired. If we really understand this, soon there will externalize the perfect answer. This will happen according to Law just as exact as the law of gravitation.

And now comes the most difficult part of it all. The thought and the idea must be abandoned into Mind. We have to establish the idea, know that we are dealing with a Law of Mind, and then let go of the idea, confident that the Law is dealing with it. It is not easy to hold and let go at the same time, and yet in a certain sense that is what we have to do. We are dealing with Something that takes ideas and makes facts out of them. As this is understood, the power is set in motion that will manifest at a level which will be absolutely identical with the mental and spiritual level of our embodiment of the idea.

Let us forever remove from our minds the thought that we shall sometime *get to* the place where God will become available. God is available, right this minute, right where we are. The everlasting Good, the ever-present, ever-available, limitless potential Power, Intelligence, and Creativeness is wherever our thought rests. All is ready to spring instantly from the invisible realm into concrete form through the pattern of our thought.

We are looking for something secure, something we can put our trust in. The thing we are all seeking is Reality. We may call it God; we may call it peace of mind; we may call it certainty, positive happiness, absolute salvation; we may call it the kingdom of heaven, but in the last analysis it is a search for that alone which is permanent. We all know enough about Reality to readily believe that if we could push farther into It there would be wonderful experiences to enjoy. Every man has at times felt if he could just do something to break the bonds within himself, open up some door which appears to be closed, he would step into completion and be instantly perfect. I am certain that when a man has harmonized himself to such a degree with Reality that in one moment's thought his Divine nature is released through him by immutable Law, it will then be impossible for him to use his power destructively. He would have to use this power for beneficent purposes only, for power is only delivered through love. The Universe cannot be divided against Itself, and we arrive at the most powerful use of thought only through constructive methods.

The right use of the creative power of Mind will bring greater results than anything we can now even dream of, for our power of imagination will increase with use. He who

87

penetrates this inner Life will find it to be birthless, deathless, fearless, eternal, happy, perfect, complete. Gradually there will dawn upon his consciousness a sense that God, the Infinite, is flowing into everything that he does. As individuals we must reeducate our minds and realize that we have an ally, a Presence and a Law, in which the past, present, and future, and all people, live and move and have their being, forever unfolding.

# 11

# TEN STEPS IN
# PERSONAL ACHIEVEMENT

How do you build a ladder of personal achievement? There are ten steps which, I believe, will help you to live happily and successfully; and in so doing, help you to help others in the glorious game of living.

So let's start with Step Number One: *Overcome negative mental attitudes.* Your basic thought here should be: "I can, if I know I can." Negative thoughts will produce negative results, while positive thinking surrounds you with an atmosphere which tends to draw good into your experience. Successful people do not permit themselves to think of failure. They occupy their minds with positive thinking.

This doesn't mean arbitrary or dogmatic thinking; rather, it means a sort of good-natured flexibility with yourself, because you are the greatest single asset you will ever possess. Practice thinking affirmatively, hopefully, about everything you do, and this must include everything: your health, your happiness, and your success. Have a bright, happy, and cheerful outlook on life.

Feed your mind with nourishing thoughts just as you feed your body with nourishing food. Feed your mind with faith, hope, and enthusiastic expectancy. Replace every doubt with a faith stronger than the doubt.

Step Number Two: *Learn to stop worrying.* In the first place, worry is an acquired habit. You didn't worry when you were a child. It is the greatest energy-waster we have; not only depressing the mind, but the physical system as well. It actually congests and retards circulation.

If you study the worry habit, you will find that you are either worrying about the past, or the outlook for the future, or the things that are happening today. Worrying about the past will not help anyone. Never look backward except to learn from experience. You do not have to carry negative experiences along with you.

Each day say to yourself: "The past is gone and I need no longer carry it along with me." Loose it and let it go and look forward to the future with hope. Build up a great idea of yourself the way you would like to be and work toward it, knowing that God is your partner and friend, and wills you to be happy. Think, feel, and live this.

Step Number Three: *Overcome any sense of inferiority.* To begin with, realize that Life has made you a little different from anyone else. You do not have to imitate. While you can, and should, learn from others, you can never be anyone but yourself, and no one can be you for you. Suppose you take this thought: "If God be for me, who can be against me?"

Do not be afraid to look yourself squarely in the face. Do not be afraid to analyze your negative thoughts so that for every denial of your good you can affirm the opposite. This thing we hear so much about, called the inferiority complex, is, after all, only a mental outlook on life. It is merely a denial that there is a Power greater than you are, a Power great enough to overcome every obstacle.

Step Number Four: *Think about your personality.* It is through your personality that all outside contacts are made. Who are you, anyway? And where did you come from? You didn't create yourself, did you? Your personality has its roots in a Divinity within you, in God, who is present everywhere. And since God has made you just a little different from all others, you need never be ashamed of yourself.

We always admire capable people, but the ones we really love are those who bring joy and happiness into our lives. A lovable person means more to us than just a person of great personal achievement—one we love, the other we admire. And it is better to be loved than it is to be admired.

This makes the whole thing rather simple. Love others and they will love you. You never have to impress people. If your attitude toward others is one of friendship, your personality will take care of itself.

Step Number Five: *Learn to make your work easy.* The one who works the easiest accomplishes the most. Of course, this doesn't mean that you are not to put the best you have into your work. It means that you can let the burden drop out of your everyday activities.

You are not carrying the world around on your shoulders; it is sustained by a Power greater than you are. And the game of living isn't intended to be a sad, heavy, dreary affair. "Easy does it," is a great motto. When the strain is taken out of what you are doing, you can do three times as much without any sense of fatigue. You will generally find that it is mostly yourself and not your work that needs to be changed.

When you get up in the morning, think, "I am doing this thing and doing it with joy." This will really produce efficiency. Here, as everywhere else, know that you are in silent partnership with God. Try to feel that you meet God in the office, in

91

the home, on the street, in people everywhere. Somehow or other, as you meet God in people and in things, God seems to· meet you.

Step Number Six: *Count your blessings.* Did you ever make an inventory of the good things in your life and write down how much you have to be thankful for? Are you glad that you are alive, glad that you have a family and friends, glad that you have the opportunity to express yourself, glad that there is a great certainty coming into your life, a feeling that you belong to the universe in which you live? When you count your blessings, don't omit the little ones. Counting your blessings will help you more than most anything else you could possibly do.

Step Number Seven: *Learn how necessary it is to forgive both yourself and others.* Did not the Great Teacher say: " . . . forgive, and ye shall be forgiven"? You cannot be a radiant personality if you hold grudges or resentments in your mind.

In taking this step of forgiveness, remember that you cannot practice this attitude with lip service alone. It must be a thing of the heart. Learn to say with James Whitcomb Riley:

> *O Thou who dost all things devise,*
> *And fashion for the best,*
> *Help us, who see with mortal eyes,*
> *To overlook the rest.*

We have to create one great blanket of forgiveness which can be summed up only in the word "love." And love alone is best.

Step Number Eight: *Getting along with others.* Only mentally sick people become hermits. If you don't get along with others, it is because you are afraid of them and because you believe they can in some way rob you of your own security. But getting along with others doesn't mean that you always agree with them. It means that such disagreements as you have are not harsh or unkind.

But how can you get along with others unless you first learn to get along with yourself? If you have been too critical of yourself, take a piece of paper and write down everything about yourself you think is admirable, and don't forget to put down your hopes and longings, because they are prophetic of what you may become. And as you think of others, think of the things that are admirable about them. When you talk of them these are the things you should talk about. People like to be appreciated.

This is more than a Pollyanna attitude. This is an ability that great and rare people possess. It is the ability you will always find in those who are surrounded by many friends. And it is as simple as this: See the good in yourself and in others, and build on this. Expect everyone to be friendly and you will lose all self-consciousness in meeting people. There are really no great and no small. We are all just human beings, trying to get along together.

Step Number Nine: *Take prayer and affirmative meditation into your personal achievement.* Prayer is not something that should be reserved for the emergencies of life alone. Your whole life should be a prayer. Prayer is both a skill and an art, and, in a certain sense, it is the mental process through which spiritual Power flows into your everyday living. Prayer hooks up the dynamo of the mind with the Power greater than you are. It is your line of communion with It.

Prayer should be affirmative. I wish you would get out your New Testament and read again all the prayers of Jesus. You ill be amazed at how affirmative they are. They are like great ecognitions of God's goodness, of life's abundance, of the peace, the poise, the power, and the love that are at the center of everything.

Step Number Ten: *Get the most out of your religion.* I have no way of knowing what your religion may be, but I am sure you have one and I know it is good. The question is not whether you or I have a religion. It is, Are we using it? Are we getting the most out of it?

If you want to get the most out of your religion you will have to share it with others. When people are gathered together in prayer and meditation, a great field of faith is created which multiplies the faith of each individual member and which can react on all who are gathered together. There is only one institution in the world where you can find this gathering together and unity of faith, and that is the institution of the church.

Your ladder is pretty complete now; but, like all ladders, it is meant to be climbed. Use it to go from where you are to where you would like to be. It is a ladder of hope, of faith, of expectancy; something that joins you with the Invisible and with all others. Climb it rung by rung and it will join the heavenly within you to its counterpart in your personal achievement.